The Cat Breed Handbook

The Cat Breed Handbook

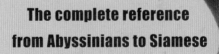

The complete reference

from Abyssinians to Siamese

Angela Rixon

Grange
BOOKS

A QUARTO BOOK

Published by Grange Books
an imprint of Grange Books Plc
The Grange
Kingsnorth Industrial Estate
Hoo, nr Rochester
Kent ME3 9ND
www.Grangebooks.co.uk

International Standard Book No. 1-84013-671-5

Conceived, designed, and produced by
Quarto Publishing plc
The Old Brewery
6 Blundell Street
London N7 9BH

QUAR.CBR

Editor: *Michelle Pickering*
Art Editor: *Anna Knight*
Designer: *Tania Field*
Assistant Art Director: *Penny Cobb*
Photographer: *Paul Forrester*

Art Director: *Moira Clinch*
Editorial Director: *Kate Kirby*
Publisher: *Piers Spence*

Manufactured by Universal Graphics Pte Ltd, Singapore
Printed by Midas Printing International Ltd, China

9 8 7 6 5 4 3 2 1

Contents

Introduction

The domestic cat enjoys a special niche in human society. It is the most enduringly popular animal portrayed throughout the world, appearing on stationery, fabrics, and ornaments. There are also numerous anthologies of poems and prose, and manuals on care and breeding.

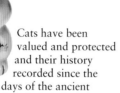

Cats have been valued and protected and their history recorded since the days of the ancient Egyptians, and although their fortunes have fluctuated from time to time, they have managed to remain virtually unchanged in size and character.

Having a pet cat in the home can be therapeutic as well as rewarding. No other pet is as clean and fastidious in its habits, or as easy to care for. Every cat is beautiful in its own way, but the very wide range of breeds, colors, and varieties of pedigree cats existing today means that every cat lover can indulge his or her particular preference.

The aim of this book is to show the diverse and interesting range of domestic felines throughout the world, exploring conformation, coat types, and patterns. It also examines the breeds' varying care requirements and their special characteristics, and acts as an introduction to the world of showing.

Showing cats

A person who breeds or shows cats is called a cat fancier. The first cat show ever recorded was held in 1598 at St. Giles Fair in Winchester, England, but the first properly benched show, with cats being placed in individual cages, took place at London's Crystal Palace in 1871. The first benched American cat show was held in Madison Square Garden, New York, in 1895.

Each country with an active band of cat fanciers has one or more governing bodies that accept cats for registration and promote cat shows. Show procedures vary, but the end result is the same. Cats are assessed by qualified judges who relate each cat's qualities to an official standard of points for its breed or variety, and then rank each cat in a class in order of merit. Non-pedigree domestic cats have a special section at most shows, and are judged on temperament, condition, and esthetic appeal.

How to use this book

Introduction to breed

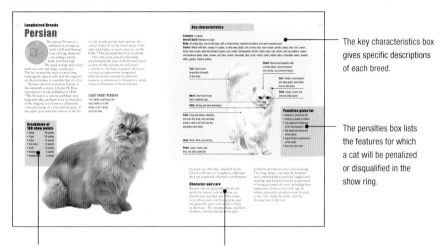

The key characteristics box gives specific descriptions of each breed.

The penalties box lists the features for which a cat will be penalized or disqualified in the show ring.

All cat associations judge each cat breed using a system of points totaling 100. Note that the points allocated can vary from association to association, so always check with the relevant governing body.

The introductory text describes the background to the breed and how it developed, followed by advice on the breed's character and care.

Breakdown of breed varieties

Each breed is broken down into color and pattern varieties.

A nose-to-tail description is given for each color and/or pattern.

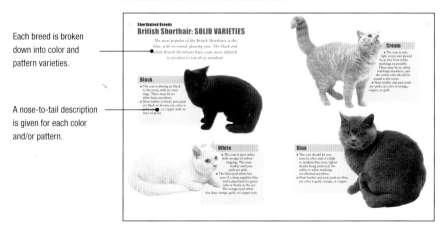

Feline Associations

Countries where pedigree cats are bred and exhibited have one or more associations or governing bodies that keep a register of cats and their lineage, and set down rules and regulations for cat shows.

CANADA
- **CCA** The Canadian Cat Association is the only all-Canadian registry, with activities centered mainly in eastern Canada.

UNITED STATES
- **ACA** The American Cat Association is a fairly small association that holds shows in the southeast and southwest of the United States.
- **ACC** The American Cat Council is a small association that has modified "English-style" shows in which exhibitors must vacate the show hall during judging.
- **CCFF** The Crown Cat Fanciers' Federation has many shows each year in the northeast and southeastern regions, and also in western Canada.
- **CFA** The Cat Fanciers' Association is the largest US association. There is a CFA show somewhere in the United States almost every weekend of the year.
- **CFF** With activities centered in the northeastern region of the United States, the Cat Fanciers' Federation is a registering body of medium size.
- **UCF** A medium-sized association, the United Cat Federation is based in the southwest of the United States.

UNITED KINGDOM

- **CA** The Cat Association of Britain keeps a register of all cats belonging to its members, and holds cat shows all over the UK.
- **GCCF** The Governing Council of the Cat Fancy has around 60 affiliated clubs and licenses cat shows all over the UK.

WORLDWIDE

- **ACFA** The American Cat Fanciers' Association has affiliated clubs in Canada and Japan, and produces a monthly news bulletin for members.
- **FIFe** Most European countries have at least two bodies for the registration of cats and licensing of shows. One body is almost certain to be affiliated to the Fédération Internationale Féline, an enormous and well-organized incorporated and chartered society that also has affiliates in countries beyond Europe. FIFe is today the largest cat body in the world.
- **TICA** The International Cat Association has shows throughout the US and affiliates in Canada and Japan.

AUSTRALASIA

- **ACF** The Australian Cat Federation is an Australia-wide recommendatory body for the breeding and showing of cats.
- **CCCA** The Co-ordinating Cat Council of Australia is also an Australia-wide recommendatory body that provides guidelines for registering and showing cats.
- **NZCF** The New Zealand Cat Fancy is the primary governing body for cat clubs in New Zealand.

Terminology

Feline associations have standardized the way in which all cats are described. To the inexperienced eye, minor variations from the "standard" may be unimportant, but for showing purposes, every detail counts in assessing a cat as a representative of its type.

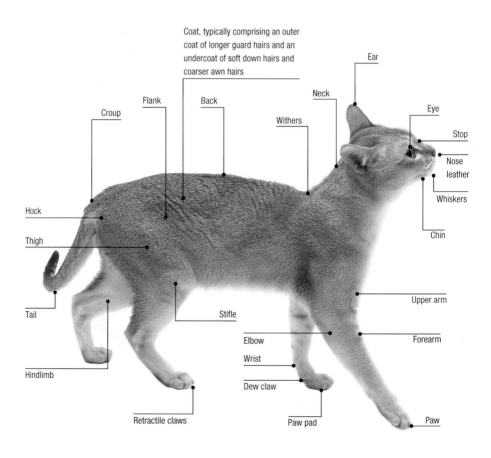

Coat, typically comprising an outer coat of longer guard hairs and an undercoat of soft down hairs and coarser awn hairs

Ear

Flank

Back

Neck

Croup

Withers

Eye

Stop

Nose leather

Whiskers

Hock

Chin

Thigh

Tail

Stifle

Upper arm

Elbow

Forearm

Wrist

Hindlimb

Dew claw

Retractile claws

Paw pad

Paw

Body Types

There are two main types of pedigree cat: those with chunky, heavyweight bodies (often called cobby) and large, round heads; and a finer type with lighter bone and longer heads. Some breeds are intermediate between the two.

HEAVYWEIGHT SHORTHAIR
Shorthaired cats with a heavy body type include the British, American, European, and Exotic Shorthairs.

HEAVYWEIGHT PERSIAN
Cats of the heavier type include Persian and other longhaired breeds.

LIGHTWEIGHT SIAMESE
Oriental cats such as the Siamese have very fine bone; very long bodies, legs, and tails; long, wedge-shaped heads; and large ears.

LIGHTWEIGHT REX
Less extreme lightweight cats include the foreign shorthairs and Rex cats.

Heads & Eyes

Most cat breeds with heavy conformation, such as the Persian and Shorthair, have large, round heads, with large, round eyes. Cats of light conformation, such as the oriental and foreign shorthaired breeds, have longer heads and narrower eyes.

PERSIAN FRONT
The head is typically round with full cheeks. The tiny ears are set wide apart.

SHORTHAIR FRONT
The head is similar to that of the Persian when viewed from the front only.

ORIENTAL FRONT
Foreign and oriental cats have long, narrow heads and large ears.

PERSIAN PROFILE
The profile is flat with a short snub nose that shows a definite "break" at eye level.

SHORTHAIR PROFILE
The profile is less flat than that of the Persian, with its short, broad nose.

ORIENTAL PROFILE
Oriental cats have long, almost Roman noses with no "break" at eye level and a flat forehead.

ROUND EYES
Persians and most shorthairs have large, round, lustrous eyes.

OVAL/ALMOND EYES
Some breed standards call for oval or almond-shaped eyes.

ORIENTAL EYES
Siamese and related breeds have eyes that slant toward the outer edge of the ear.

Coat Types

Pedigree cats have diverse variations of coat types, ranging from the profuse pelt of the Persian to the sleek coat of the Siamese. Between the two extremes are the soft, silky coats of the longhaired foreign breeds and the thick, dense coats of some shorthairs.

PERSIAN
Long, soft coat with profuse down hairs nearly as long as the guard hairs, producing a typically long and full coat.

MAINE COON
Long, silky coat, heavier and less uniform than that of the Persian due to less uniform and denser down hairs.

SHORTHAIR
Shorthair coats are very variable, ranging from the British and American breeds to the foreign shorthairs.

SPHYNX
Apparently hairless, the Sphynx does have a light covering of down hairs on some areas of the body.

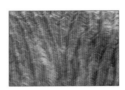

CORNISH REX
The tightly curled coat of the Cornish Rex is caused by the absence of guard hairs and short awn hairs.

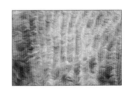

DEVON REX
The genetically modified guard and awn hairs in this breed closely resemble down hairs.

AMERICAN WIREHAIR
Different from the two Rex coats, the wirehair has crimped awn hairs and waved guard hairs.

ORIENTAL
In the Siamese and oriental breeds, the coat is short, fine, and close lying.

Solids & Bicolors

Cats of solid-colored, or self-colored, breeds must be of a single color with no pattern or shading. Bicolor cats are of two colors: a varietal color and white, with between half and two-thirds of the coat being colored. There must be no tabby markings in the solid-colored areas.

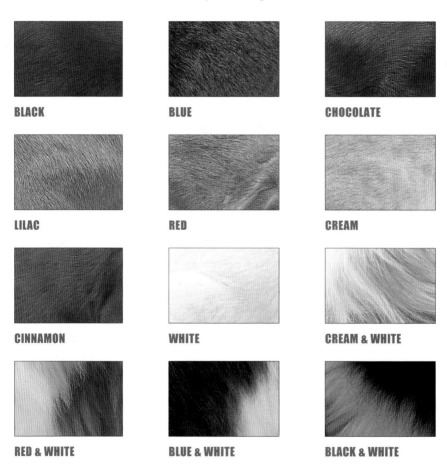

BLACK

BLUE

CHOCOLATE

LILAC

RED

CREAM

CINNAMON

WHITE

CREAM & WHITE

RED & WHITE

BLUE & WHITE

BLACK & WHITE

Tipped Colors

In the unusually colored tipped breeds, different effects are produced by a proportion of each hair having a colored tip while the rest of the hair is of a paler color. Smoke, tabby, and shaded coats are found in all the usual solid colors.

CHINCHILLA SILVER

Tipped cats such as the Chinchilla have tipping at the very ends of the hairs, producing a sparkling effect.

CHINCHILLA GOLDEN

In golden varieties, the white base coat of the silver varieties is replaced by a tawny yellow color.

RED SHADED

Tipping that extends farther down the hair shaft than in Chinchilla cats produces the more strongly colored shaded varieties. Shaded coats are found in many different colors.

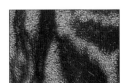

BROWN TABBY

Variable bands of color in different areas of the coat give rise to tabby effects in several colors.

BLUE SMOKE

Tipping extending almost to the white hair roots produces the smoke coat. Again, many different colors of smoke coats are found.

Colorpoints

Colorpointed cats have pale coats with the main color restricted to the points—face, ears, legs, and tail. This is known as the Himalayan pattern. Lynx point cats have tabby markings on the points, while tortie point cats have tortoiseshell markings on the points.

SEAL POINT

BLUE POINT

RED POINT

CREAM POINT

LILAC POINT

CHOCOLATE POINT

SEAL LYNX POINT

BLUE LYNX POINT

RED LYNX POINT

SEAL TORTIE POINT

CHOCOLATE TORTIE POINT

Multiple Colors

Cats come in coats of many colors and patterns apart from those already described. Tortoiseshells (often called torties for convenience) are the most common. Torbies, which are also known as patched tabbies, are a mixture of tortoiseshell and tabby patterns.

TORTOISESHELL
Black body color with patches of red and/or light red.

CHOCOLATE TORTIE
Chocolate body color with patches of light red.

LILAC TORTIE
Lilac body color with patches of pale cream. Also known as lilac-cream.

BLUE-CREAM
Dilute form of tortoiseshell, with blue body color and patches of cream. Also known as blue tortie.

CALICO
White body color with patches of black and red tortoiseshell. Also known as tortie and white.

DILUTE CALICO
White body color with patches of blue and cream tortoiseshell. Also known as blue tortie and white.

BROWN TORBIE
Coppery brown base coat, black tabby markings, and patches of red and/or light red tortoiseshell.

BLUE TORBIE
Pale bluish ivory base coat, deep blue tabby markings, and patches of cream tortoiseshell.

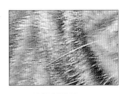

SILVER TORBIE
Pale silver base coat, black tabby markings, and patches of red and/or light red tortoiseshell.

Tabby Patterns

The natural color of the domestic cat is tabby, which may be one
of four basic patterns. The wild type is ticked tabby (agouti),
and the other tabby patterns are mackerel (striped),
classic (marbled or blotched), and spotted.
Each pattern can be found in any color.

Ticked tabby

- Each hair of the coat is ticked with two or three bands of color to produce the effect commonly seen in wild rabbits.
- There are clear tabby bar markings on the legs and tail.

Mackerel tabby

- Markings resemble narrow pencil lines. The legs and tail are evenly barred, and there are several distinct narrow necklaces around the neck.
- Lines run together along the spine to form a dark saddle, and fine, pencil-like markings run down each side of the body from the spine.

Classic tabby

- The legs and tail are evenly barred, and there are several unbroken necklaces on the neck and upper chest. Shoulder markings resemble a butterfly, with upper and lower wings outlined and marked with dots inside.
- The back is marked with a spine line and a parallel line on each side, all separated by stripes of the coat's ground color. A large solid blotch on each side of the body is encircled by one or more unbroken rings, and the side markings are the same on both sides of the body.

Head markings

- For all tabby patterns, the head has frown marks forming a letter "M," and an unbroken line running back from the outer corner of each eye.
- There are swirl markings on the cheeks, and vertical lines running over the back of the head to the shoulder markings.

Spotted tabby

- The spots can be round, oval, oblong, or rosette-shaped. The legs are clearly spotted, and the tail spotted or with broken rings.
- Spotted cats are penalized when the spots are not distinct, and for having bars, except on the head.

Cat Care

*The domestic cat is quite easy to care for within the confines
of the home. It must be provided with some basic equipment,
such as feeding and drinking bowls, a comfortable bed,
a litter tray, and a scratching post.*

Giving a cat the correct care is basically a question of common sense. A cat must be given a clean, warm environment in which to live; the correct amount of suitable, nourishing food; constant access to fresh, clean drinking water; and facilities for play and exercise.

A cat should have a bed of its own in a quiet, secluded place, and it should be left in peace to sleep for undisturbed periods during the day. Meals should be fed regularly, on clean dishes, and any food not eaten within a reasonable time should be removed and disposed of. Cats will not eat stale food. Fresh water should be provided every day and left down for the cat to drink whenever it wishes.

Even if the cat has access to the outdoors, it should be provided with a toilet tray and fresh litter at all times. It is more hygienic for the cat's wastes to be disposed of than for it to soil the yard. Various types of litter boxes are available, some with hooded lids. The litter tray should be washed and

dried when the litter is changed, and sterilized with diluted household bleach or a safe disinfectant recommended by the veterinarian.

Cats need to strop their claws from time to time, to keep them in good condition and to remove any loose scale. Various types of scratching posts are available, from simple cardboard strips to ingenious constructions of shelves and posts covered with rope or carpet. A cat prefers to strop its claws on an upright post rather than one laid flat on the floor.

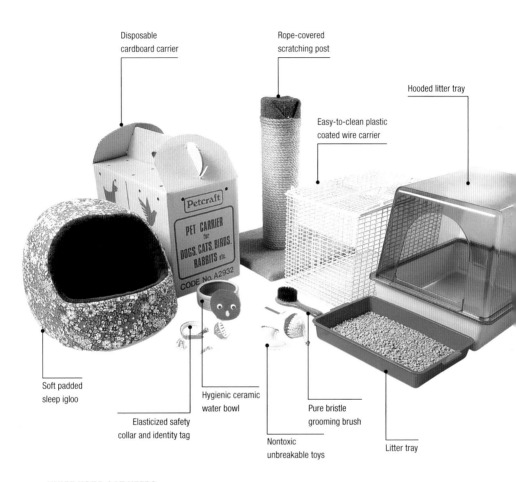

Disposable
cardboard carrier

Rope-covered
scratching post

Hooded litter tray

Easy-to-clean plastic
coated wire carrier

Petcraft

PET CARRIER
for
DOGS, CATS, BIRDS,
RABBITS etc.

CODE No. A2932

Soft padded
sleep igloo

Hygienic ceramic
water bowl

Pure bristle
grooming brush

Elasticized safety
collar and identity tag

Nontoxic
unbreakable toys

Litter tray

WHAT YOUR CAT NEEDS
A vast range of equipment is available for
the pet cat, and in a broad price band.

Health & Grooming

Keeping your cat healthy is mainly a matter of common sense and proper husbandry. A regular regime of care will help your cat to stay in good condition and be less likely to become ill.

Health regime

Follow this regime and check your cat's appearance and behavior regularly. If you notice any problems, seek veterinary attention.

Daily

- Feed a well-balanced diet of good-quality food.
- Provide fresh water in a clean container.
- Dispose of soiled litter; clean toilet tray; check cat's stools (and urine if possible) for any sign of abnormality.
- Groom the cat according to its coat type and hair length.

- In free-ranging cats, check the coat for the staining that could indicate diarrhea and for foreign bodies; check the feet for sore or cracked pads; check all over for signs of fighting.

Weekly

- Examine ears and coat for parasites.
- Check mouth and throat; clean teeth if necessary.

Monthly

- Check the cat all over with your fingers, feeling for any lumps, bumps, lesions, or foreign bodies.

Six-monthly

- Check the cat's records to see if blood tests or vaccinations are due and mark the dates in your diary.

Yearly

- Have a complete veterinary check carried out in conjunction with an annual booster vaccination program.

Grooming

Most cats benefit from grooming, and longhaired breeds such as the Persian must be groomed daily to keep the full coat in good condition and to prevent the soft undercoat from matting. Start grooming routines when the cat is very young so that it becomes accustomed to being brushed.

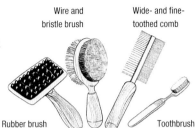

Wire and bristle brush

Wide- and fine-toothed comb

Rubber brush

Toothbrush

Grooming a longhaired cat

1 Apply grooming powder to the coat.

2 Work the powder into the coat, starting from the tail and moving toward the head.

3 Brush the coat thoroughly, removing the powder and lifting the coat away from the skin.

4 Use a wide-toothed comb from tail to head to make sure there are no tangles; pay particular attention to the underparts.

5 Clean the eyes, nostrils, and inside the ear flaps with a series of moist swabs or small brush.

1   2   3   4   5

Grooming a shorhaired cat

1 Remove dust, loose hairs, and any debris or parasites, using a metal fine-toothed comb from head to tail.

2 A rubber brush may be used for cats with thick, short coats.

3 A soft-bristled brush is best for cats with very fine, short coats.

4 Buff the coat with a special grooming mitt, a piece of silk or velvet, or a chamois leather.

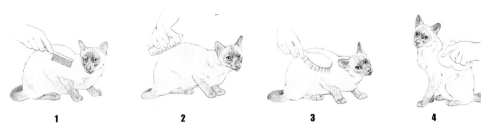

1   2   3   4

Longhaired Breeds

Persian

The typical Persian is a substantial, strong cat, with a full and flowing coat of long, dense fur concealing a sturdy body and thick legs.

The head is large and round with tiny ears and large, round eyes. The fur around the neck is extra long, forming the typical ruff, and the long hair on the tail makes it resemble that of a fox.

Persian cats first arrived in Europe in the sixteenth century. Charles H. Ross reported in a book published in 1868: "The Persian is a variety with hair very long and silky; perhaps more so than that of the Angora; it is however differently coloured, being of a fine uniform grey on the upper part with the texture of the fur as soft as silk and the lustre glossy; the colour fades off on the lower parts of the sides and fades, or nearly does so, on the belly." This preceded the first cat shows.

Over the years, selective breeding standardized the type of the Persian breed so that all the varieties would closely conform to one basic standard. However, various cat associations designated different points awards for different features as incentives for breeders to work toward refinement of those features.

LILAC TABBY PERSIAN
The tabby markings are less distinct in the dilute color range, such as lilac.

Breakdown of 100 show points

• Head	30 points
• Type	20 points
• Color	20 points
• Eye color	10 points
• Coat	10 points
• Balance	5 points
• Refinement	5 points

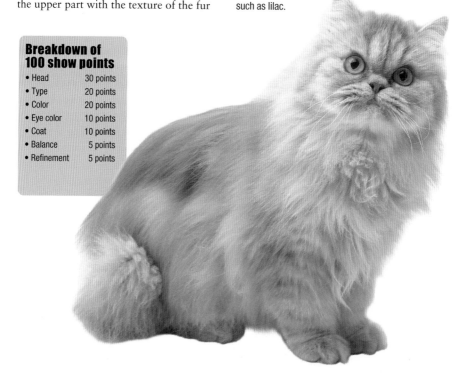

Key characteristics

Category Longhair.

Overall build Medium to large.

Body Of cobby type, low on the legs, with a broad chest, massive shoulders, and well-muscled back.

Colors White with blue, orange or copper, or odd eyes; black, red, cream, blue, blue-cream; smoke: black, blue, red, cream, tortie, blue-cream; shell and shaded cameo: red, cream, tortoiseshell; bicolor: black, blue, red, cream, and van pattern; classic and mackerel tabby: silver, brown, red, blue, cream, chocolate, lilac; tortie, torbie, calico, dilute calico; chinchilla: silver, shaded silver, golden, shaded golden.

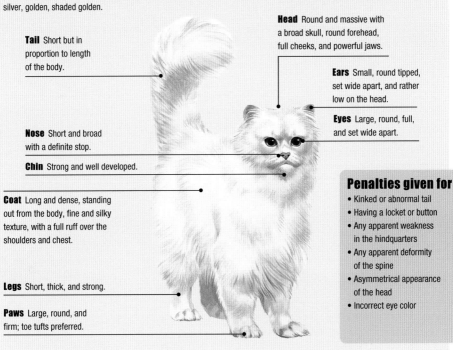

Tail Short but in proportion to length of the body.

Head Round and massive with a broad skull, round forehead, full cheeks, and powerful jaws.

Ears Small, round tipped, set wide apart, and rather low on the head.

Nose Short and broad with a definite stop.

Eyes Large, round, full, and set wide apart.

Chin Strong and well developed.

Coat Long and dense, standing out from the body, fine and silky texture, with a full ruff over the shoulders and chest.

Legs Short, thick, and strong.

Paws Large, round, and firm; toe tufts preferred.

Penalties given for

- Kinked or abnormal tail
- Having a locket or button
- Any apparent weakness in the hindquarters
- Any apparent deformity of the spine
- Asymmetrical appearance of the head
- Incorrect eye color

Persians are officially classified by the GCCF in Britain as Longhairs, although they are popularly referred to as Persians.

Character and care

Persian cats are generally placid and gentle by nature, and as kittens are playful and mischievous. They make very affectionate and loving pets, and are generally quiet and restful to have in the home. The females make excellent mothers, and the kittens rarely give problems during lactation and weaning. The long, dense coat must be brushed and combed daily to prevent tangles and matting, and kittens must be accustomed to being groomed all over, including their underparts, from a very early age. In adults, particular attention must be paid to the ruff, under the belly, and the flowing hair of the tail.

Persian: SOLID VARIETIES

In the UK, each color type of the Persian is considered an individual breed and these breeds are no longer called Persians, but Longhairs. In the US, however, all are considered Persians of differing color types.

White

- The coat is pure, glistening white without any markings or shading. Nose leather and paw pads are pink.
- There are three varieties: blue eyed; copper eyed (US) or orange eyed (UK); and odd eyed, with one eye of deep blue, the other of copper or orange. Blue-eyed whites are sometimes deaf due to a genetic factor; odd-eyed whites may be deaf in the ear adjacent to the blue eye.

Black

- The coat is dense, coal black from roots to tips of hair, free from any tinge, markings, or shading of any kind, and with no white hair.
- Nose leather is black; paw pads are black or brown; eye color is brilliant copper (US) or copper or deep orange (UK), with no green rim.

Red

- The coat is deep, rich, clear, brilliant red without markings, shading, or ticking. The lips and chin are the same color as the coat.
- Nose leather and paw pads are brick red; eye color is brilliant copper (US) or deep copper (UK).

Cream

- In the US, the coat is required to be an even shade of buff cream, with lighter shades preferred. In the UK, the coat should be pale to medium in color. FIFe requires pale, pastel cream with no warm tone. In all cases, the color must be sound from root to tip, without any markings or shading.
  - Nose leather and paw pads are pink; eye color is brilliant copper (US) or deep copper (UK).

Persian: SOLID VARIETIES *continued*

Blue

- The coat is an even tone of blue from nose to tail tip, and sound from roots to tips of hair. Any shade of blue is allowed, but in the US lighter shades are preferred. The coat must be free from all markings, shading, or white hairs.
- Nose leather and paw pads are blue; eye color is brilliant copper (US) or deep orange or copper (UK), without any trace of green.

Blue-cream

- In the US, the coat is required to be blue with clearly defined patches of solid cream, well broken on both body and extremities. In the UK, the coat should consist of pastel shades of blue and cream, softly intermingled. FIFe requires light blue gray and pale cream, patched and/or mingled, with both colors evenly distributed over the body and extremities.
- Eye color is brilliant copper (US) or deep copper or orange (UK).

Persian: CAMEO VARIETIES

Cameo Persians have a white undercoat tipped with color. There are three intensities: shell is very pale and has a sparkling appearance; shaded is darker with a dazzling sheen; and smoke is darker still.

Cream cameo

- The white coat has a mantle of cream tipping on the face, back, sides, and tail. The color graduates from dark on the ridge of the back to white on the chest, stomach, under the tail, and on the chin. The legs are the same tone as the face.
- Eye rims are rose; eye color is brilliant copper.

Red cameo

- The white coat is tipped with red on the head, back, flanks, and tail, graduating from a darker color on the ridge to white on the chest, stomach, under the tail, and on the chin. The face and legs may be tipped, but less so on shell cameos.
- Eye rims, nose leather, and paw pads are rose; eye color is brilliant copper.

Blue-cream cameo

- The blue- and cream-tipped hairs of this variety may be of any intensity, overlaying a white undercoat. In the US, well-defined patches of cream-tipped hair are required among the blue tipping; in the UK, blue and cream can be softly intermingled.
- Eye color is brilliant copper.

Tortoiseshell cameo

- The white coat is tipped with black, with well-defined patches of red- and light red-tipped hairs in the tortoiseshell pattern on the head, back, flanks, and tail. The face and legs may be tipped, and a blaze of red or light red tipping on the face is desirable.
- Eye color is brilliant copper.

Persian: SMOKE VARIETIES

The smoke Persian is known as "the cat of contrasts," and though rare, is generally of excellent longhair type. In recent years, the rare smoke Persian has been bred in colors other than the original black.

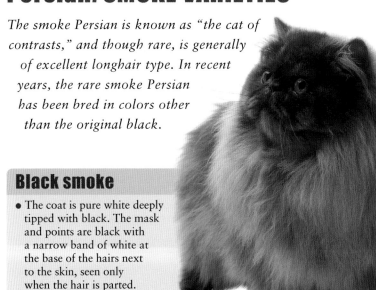

Black smoke

- The coat is pure white deeply tipped with black. The mask and points are black with a narrow band of white at the base of the hairs next to the skin, seen only when the hair is parted.
- The ruff and ear tufts are light silver; nose leather and paw pads are black; eye color is brilliant copper (US) or orange or copper (UK).

Blue smoke

- The white coat is deeply tipped with blue. The mask and points are blue with a narrow band of white at the base of the hairs next to the skin.
- The ruff and ear tufts are white; nose leather and paw pads are blue; eye color is brilliant copper (US) or orange or copper (UK).

Red smoke

- The coat is white deeply tipped with red. The mask and points are red, with a narrow band of white at the base of the hairs next to the skin.
- The ruff and ear tufts are white; eye rims, nose leather, and paw pads are rose; eye color is brilliant copper.

Cream smoke

- This variety is a dilute version of the red smoke Persian. The cream coloring fades to white on the sides and flanks.
- The ruff and ear tufts are white; eye rims, nose leather, and paw pads are rose; eye color is brilliant copper.

Tortoiseshell smoke

- The coat is white deeply tipped with black, with clearly defined, unbrindled patches of red and light red hairs in the tortoiseshell pattern. The face and ears are tortoiseshell patterned with a narrow band of white at the base of the hairs next to the skin, seen only when the hair is parted.
- A blaze of red or light red tipping on the face is desirable; ruff and ear tufts are white; eye color is brilliant copper.

Blue-cream smoke

- The coat is white deeply tipped with blue, with clearly defined, unbrindled patches of cream. The face and ears are similarly patterned, with a narrow band of white at the base of the hairs next to the skin, seen only when the hair is parted.
- A blaze of cream tipping on the face is desirable; ruff and ear tufts are white; eye color is brilliant copper.

Persian: BICOLOR VARIETIES

The coat of the bicolor Persian combines a solid color with white: black and white, blue and white, red and white, or cream and white. Van patterns are also accepted in the same color combinations.

BLACK & WHITE BICOLOR

This massive cat has very good markings, particularly the desired white "collar."

Bicolor

- In the US, cats are required to have white legs and paws; white on the chest, underbody, and muzzle; and an inverted "V" of white on the face is desirable. White is also allowed under the tail and as a marking resembling a collar around the neck.
- In the UK, the patches of color should be clear and evenly distributed, with not more than two-thirds of the coat being colored, and not more than half of the coat being white. The face must be patched with color and white.

BLUE & WHITE BICOLOR

The inverted "V" on the face of this fine Persian is one of the features required for exhibition of this variety in the US.

RED & WHITE BICOLOR

Red and white, and cream and white, bicolor cats should be free from any shading in the colored areas of their coats.

CREAM & WHITE BICOLOR

In the bicolor, the face is required to show both colored and white areas.

Van bicolor

- The distribution of color is quite different from that of the bicolor. The van bicolor is basically a white cat with the color confined to the extremities.
- One or two small colored patches on the body are allowed.

Persian: TABBY VARIETIES

The tabby Persian is accepted in classic and mackerel patterns. A wide variety of colors are shown in the US, while only three color varieties are shown in the UK—silver, brown, and red.

Silver tabby

- The coat, including lips and chin, is pure pale silver with dense black markings.
- Nose leather is brick red; paw pads are black; eye color is green or hazel.

Red tabby

- The coat, including lips and chin, is red with deep, rich red markings.
- Nose leather is brick red; paw pads are black or brown; eye color is brilliant copper.

Brown tabby

- The coat is brilliant coppery brown with dense black markings. The lips and chin are the same color as the rings around the eyes. The backs of the legs should be black from paw to heel.
- Nose leather is brick red; paw pads are black or brown; eye color is copper (US) or hazel (UK).

Blue tabby

- The coat, including lips and chin, is pale bluish ivory with very deep blue markings that afford a good contrast with the ground color. A warm fawn patina covers the whole cat.
  - Nose leather is old rose; paw pads are rose; eye color is copper.

Torbie

- The torbie Persian is a cat in which the tabby pattern in the main coat color is overlaid with a shading of red.
  - Both tabby and tortoiseshell areas should remain clearly visible.

Persian: TORTOISESHELL VARIETIES

Tortoiseshell cats have always been popular as pets.
Tortoiseshell-and-white cats are referred to as calico cats
in the US. Once known as chintz cats in the UK, they
are now simply called tortoiseshell and whites.

Tortoiseshell

- The coat is black with unbrindled and clearly defined patches of red and light red on both the body and extremities.
- A blaze of red or light red on the face is desirable. Eye color is brilliant copper.

Chocolate tortie

- The black and red areas of the tortie are replaced by warm chocolate and light red.
- A blaze of red or light red on the face is desirable. Eye color is brilliant copper.

Calico

- The coat is white with unbrindled patches of black and red, with the colors well distributed and interspersed with white. White is predominant on the underparts.
- Eye color is brilliant copper (US) or deep orange or copper (UK).

Dilute calico

- The coat is white with unbrindled patches of blue and cream; white is predominant on the underparts. The patches of color are required to be distinct and free from scattered white hairs.
- Eye color is brilliant copper (US) or deep orange or copper (UK).

Persian: CHINCHILLA VARIETIES

Perhaps the most glamorous of the longhairs, the chinchilla Persian has a sparkling appearance. Shaded varieties are generally darker.

Chinchilla silver

- The coat is pure white tipped with black on the head, back, flanks, and tail. The legs may be slightly tipped. The chin, ear tufts, chest, and stomach are pure white, and the rims of the eyes, lips, and nose are outlined with black.
- Nose leather is brick red; paw pads are black; eye color is green or blue green.

Shaded silver

- The coat is white tipped with black down the face, sides, and tail, graduating to white on the chin, chest, stomach, and under the tail. The legs are the same tone as the face, and the rims of the eyes, lips, and nose are outlined with black.
- Nose leather is brick red; paw pads are black; eye color is green or blue green.

Chinchilla golden

- The coat is rich, warm cream sufficiently tipped with seal brown on the head, back, flanks, and tail to give a golden appearance. The legs may be slightly tipped, and the rims of the eyes, lips, and nose are outlined with seal brown.
- Nose leather is deep rose; paw pads are seal brown; eye color is green or blue green.

Shaded golden

- The coat is rich, warm cream with a mantle of seal brown tipping down the face, sides, and tail, graduating to cream on the chin, chest, stomach, and under the tail. The legs are the same tone as the face. The rims of the eyes, lips, and nose are outlined with seal brown.
- Nose leather is deep rose; paw pads are seal brown; eye color is green or blue green.

Himalayan

This breed is a cat of true Persian type with the markings first known in Siamese cats, where the true coat color is restricted to the cooler areas of the cat's body, known as the points. These include the face, or mask, the ears, the legs and paws, and the tail. This coloring is produced by a recessive gene, often referred to as the Himalayan factor, hence the name used for Persian cats of this pattern.

The first crosses between Siamese and Persian cats were made in Sweden as long ago as 1922. Further experimental matings were made in the US during the 1920s and 1930s, but it was not until the 1950s that breeders on both sides of the Atlantic, working with carefully planned breeding programs, produced cats with the desired type and coat pattern. In 1955, Britain's GCCF issued a breed number and approved a standard of points for the Himalayan-patterned Persians, but designated them as Colorpoint Longhairs. In the US, recognition of the Himalayan was approved by the CFA in 1957, and by the 1960s all other American associations had accepted the variety.

Breakdown of 100 show points

• Head	30 points
• Type	20 points
• Coat	10 points
• Body color	10 points
• Points color	10 points
• Eye color	10 points
• Balance	5 points
• Refinement	5 points

RED TABBY POINT HIMALAYAN

In the red series, some slight shading similar to that of the points color may be seen on the pale body.

Category Longhair.

Overall build Medium or large.

Body Of stocky type, low on the legs, with a deep chest, and equally massive across the shoulders and rump.

Colors Seal point, blue point, chocolate point, lilac point, red point, cream point, blue-cream point, seal tortie point, chocolate tortie point, seal tabby point, blue tabby point, chocolate tabby point, lilac tabby point, red tabby point, cream tabby point, blue-cream tabby point, seal torbie point, chocolate torbie point, chocolate kashmir, lilac kashmir, lilac-cream kashmir.

Head Round and massive, with very broad skull, round face, and set on a short, thick neck; full cheeks.

Ears Small, round tipped, tilted slightly forward, and set far apart on the head.

Tail Short, but in proportion to body length; hair forms a "brush."

Coat Long and thick over the entire body, of fine texture, and glossy; immense ruff around the neck and extending between the forelegs. Long tufts on the ears and between the toes.

Eyes Large, full, round, and set far apart.

Nose Short, broad, with a stop.

Chin Full and well developed.

Legs Short, thick, and heavy; straight forelegs.

Paws Large, round, and firm; toes not splayed.

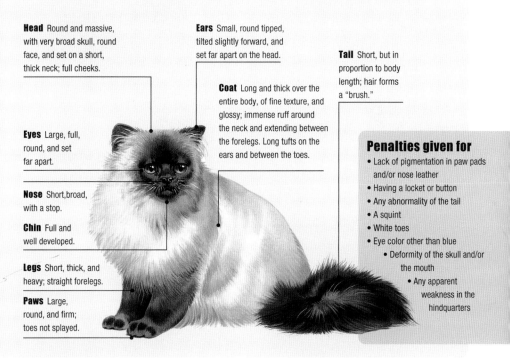

Penalties given for

- Lack of pigmentation in paw pads and/or nose leather
- Having a locket or button
- Any abnormality of the tail
- A squint
- White toes
- Eye color other than blue
- Deformity of the skull and/or the mouth
- Any apparent weakness in the hindquarters

Character and care

The character of the Himalayan combines the best traits of the cats used in its creation—the Siamese and the Persian. It is generally a little livelier and more entertaining than its solid-colored Persian cousins, but less vocal and boisterous than the typical Siamese. The precocious breeding tendencies of its Siamese ancestry have been passed on, with Himalayan females coming into season and "calling" as early as eight months of age, though the males often do not reach maturity until they are 18 months old.

Regular grooming is essential to keep the long, full coat in good condition, paying particular attention to the underparts, between the hind and fore legs, under the tail, and around the neck, thoroughly brushing out the ruff.

Himalayan: SOLID POINTS

*The coloring on all of the points should
match in tone and be free from shadow
markings or any patchiness.*

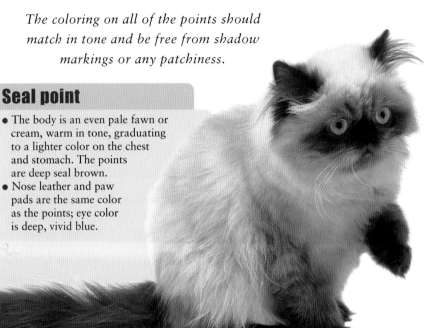

Seal point

- The body is an even pale fawn or cream, warm in tone, graduating to a lighter color on the chest and stomach. The points are deep seal brown.
- Nose leather and paw pads are the same color as the points; eye color is deep, vivid blue.

Blue point

- The body is bluish-white, cold in tone, graduating to white on the chest and stomach. The points are blue.
  - Nose leather and paw pads are slate gray; eye color is deep, vivid blue.

Cream point

- The body is creamy white with no shading. The points are buff cream and should have no apricot tinges.
- Nose leather and paw pads are flesh pink or salmon coral; eye color is deep, vivid blue.

Red point

- The body is creamy white. The points color varies from deep orange flame to deep red.
- Nose leather and paw pads are flesh or coral pink; eye color is deep, vivid blue.

Chocolate point

- The body is ivory with no shading. The points are milk chocolate and warm in tone.
- Nose leather and paw pads are cinnamon pink; eye color is deep, vivid blue.

Lilac point

- The body is glacial white with no shading. The points are frosty gray with a pinkish tone.
- Nose leather and paw pads are lavender pink; eye color is deep, vivid blue.

Himalayan: TABBY POINTS

Tabby-pointed varieties should have a clear "M" marking on the forehead, spotted whisker pads, and typical "glasses" marks around the eyes. The inner ear is light, and there is a "thumbprint" on the back of the outer ear. The tips of the ears and tail should match.

Seal tabby point

- The body is pale cream to fawn and warm in tone. The points are beige brown with darker brown tabby markings.
- Nose leather is seal or brick red; paw pads are seal brown; eye color is deep, vivid blue.

Blue tabby point

- The body is bluish white and cold in tone. The points are light silvery blue with darker blue tabby markings.
- Nose leather is blue or brick red; paw pads are blue; eye color is deep, vivid blue.

Chocolate tabby point

- The body is ivory. The points are warm fawn ticked with milk chocolate markings.
- Nose leather and paw pads are cinnamon pink; eye color is deep, vivid blue.

Red tabby point

- The body is creamy white. The points are light red ticked with deeper red tabby markings.
- Nose leather and paw pads are flesh or coral pink; eye color is deep, vivid blue.

Lilac tabby point

- The body is glacial white. The points are frosty gray ticked with darker frosty gray tabby markings.
- Nose leather and paw pads are lavender pink; eye color is deep, vivid blue.

Blue-cream point

- The body is bluish white or creamy white graduating to white on the chest and stomach. The points are blue with patches of cream.
- Nose leather and paw pads are slate gray or pink, or a combination of slate gray and pink mottling; eye color is deep, vivid blue.

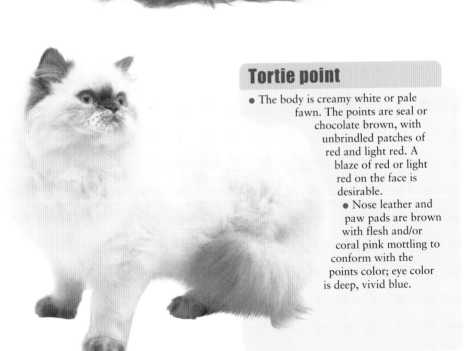

Tortie point

- The body is creamy white or pale fawn. The points are seal or chocolate brown, with unbrindled patches of red and light red. A blaze of red or light red on the face is desirable.
- Nose leather and paw pads are brown with flesh and/or coral pink mottling to conform with the points color; eye color is deep, vivid blue.

Himalayan: KASHMIR VARIETIES

Kashmir is the breed name used by some associations in the US for the solid-colored chocolate and lilac Persians; others group them with the Himalayans. In the UK, they are called the Chocolate Longhair and the Lilac Longhair.

Chocolate kashmir

- The coat is rich, warm chocolate brown, sound from the roots to the tips of the hair, and free from markings, shading, or white hairs.
- Nose leather and paw pads are brown; eye color is brilliant copper (US) or deep orange or copper (UK).

Lilac kashmir

- The coat is rich, warm lavender with a pinkish tone, sound from the roots to the tips of the hair, and free from markings, shading, or white hairs.
- Nose leather and paw pads are pink; eye color is brilliant copper (US) or pale orange (UK).

Lilac-cream kashmir

- This variety, with patched or intermingled lilac and light cream hairs, was created when the red or orange genetic factor was added to some breeding programs.
- Nose leather and paw pads are pink; eye color is brilliant copper (US) or pale orange (UK).

Semi-longhaired Breeds

Birman

Also known as the Sacred Cat of Burma, the Birman is quite unrelated to the Burmese, despite the similarity in names. It is a unique breed, for although it bears a superficial resemblance to the Himalayan, or Colorpoint Longhair, it has stark white paws on all four feet. Its coat is silky, more like that of the Turkish Angora than the Himalayan, and its body type differs from that of the Persian, being longer and less cobby.

Legends abound explaining the origins of this beautiful breed, and one in particular attempts to explain the Birman's coloring. Before the time of Buddha, the Khmer people built temples in honor of their gods. One such temple was raised to Tsun-Kyan-Kse, where a golden statue of the goddess so named was worshipped. In the early 1900s the temple was raided, but it was saved by Major Gordon Russell and Monsieur Auguste Pavie. As a gesture of thanks, a pair of temple cats were sent to the two men, now living in France. The male cat died en route, but the female arrived safely and gave birth to kittens that founded the Birman breed in Europe.

Breakdown of 100 show points

- Head   30 points
- Type   25 points
- Color   25 points
- Coat   10 points
- Eye color   10 points

SEAL TORTIE POINT BIRMAN

Seal brown overlaid and intermingled with red and light red produce the tortoiseshell coloring of this Birman.

Category Longhair.

Overall build Medium. Males are more massive than females.

Body Fairly long but not stocky.

Colors Solid points and tabby points in seal, blue, chocolate, lilac, red, cream; tortie points and torbie points in seal, blue, chocolate, lilac.

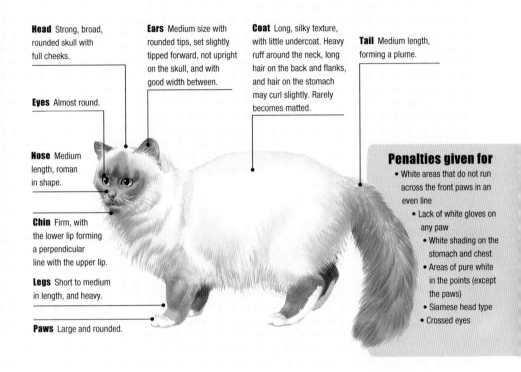

Head Strong, broad, rounded skull with full cheeks.

Ears Medium size with rounded tips, set slightly tipped forward, not upright on the skull, and with good width between.

Coat Long, silky texture, with little undercoat. Heavy ruff around the neck, long hair on the back and flanks, and hair on the stomach may curl slightly. Rarely becomes matted.

Tail Medium length, forming a plume.

Eyes Almost round.

Nose Medium length, roman in shape.

Chin Firm, with the lower lip forming a perpendicular line with the upper lip.

Legs Short to medium in length, and heavy.

Paws Large and rounded.

Penalties given for
- White areas that do not run across the front paws in an even line
- Lack of white gloves on any paw
- White shading on the stomach and chest
- Areas of pure white in the points (except the paws)
- Siamese head type
- Crossed eyes

Character and care

The Birman is an inquisitive and affectionate cat, with a rather aloof appearance, giving the impression that it is fully aware of its mystical origins. Unlike many other longhaired breeds, the Birman matures early, and the females often start to "call" as early as seven months of age.

The Birman coat is silkier and less dense than that of the Persian. It is comparatively easy to keep well groomed with regular brushing and combing. The white gloves and gauntlets must be kept free from staining by regular washing, careful drying, and the application of white grooming powder that is rubbed in, then completely brushed out, leaving the white areas spotlessly clean.

Birman: SOLID POINTS

*Kittens are born almost white all over, with
the points color starting to develop at the edges
of the ears and on the tail within a few days.
The eye color is blue for all varieties,
the deeper and more violet the better.*

Seal point

- The body is even fawn to pale
cream, warm in tone, graduating
to a lighter color on the stomach
and chest. The points are deep
seal brown, except for gloves
that are pure white.
- Nose leather should match the
points; paw pads are pink.

Blue point

- The body is bluish white, cold in tone, graduating to almost white on the stomach and chest. The points are deep blue, except for gloves that are pure white.
  - Nose leather is slate; paw pads are pink.

Chocolate point

- The body is ivory with no shading. The points are milk chocolate and warm in tone, except for gloves that are pure white.
- Nose leather is cinnamon pink; paw pads are pink.

Birman: SOLID POINTS *continued*

Lilac point

- The body has a cold glacial tone verging on white with no shading. The points are frosty gray with a pinkish tinge, except for gloves that are pure white.
  - Nose leather is lavender pink; paw pads are pink.

Red point

- The body is creamy white. The points are bright warm orange, except for gloves that are white.
- Nose leather and paw pads are pink.

Cream point

- The body is creamy white. The points are pastel cream, except for gloves that are white.
- Nose leather and paw pads are pink.

Birman: TABBY & TORTOISESHELL POINTS

Tabby Birmans are accepted in the same six basic colors as solid point Birmans. Tortie and torbie Birmans are accepted in seal, blue, chocolate, and lilac.

Seal tabby point

- The body is beige, with dark seal tabby points, except for gloves that are white.
- Nose leather is brick red, pink, or seal brown; paw pads are pink.

Seal tortie point

- The body is beige, graduating to fawn. The points are seal brown patched or mingled with red and/or light red, except for gloves that are white.
- Nose leather is pink and/or seal.

Seal torbie point

- The body is beige. The points have tabby markings in seal brown patched or mingled with red and/or light red, except for gloves that are white.
- Nose leather is seal, brick red, or pink, or seal mottled with brick red or pink.

Birman: TABBY & TORTOISESHELL POINTS *continued*

Blue tabby point

- The body is bluish white, with blue gray tabby points, except for gloves that are white.
- Nose leather is old rose or blue gray.

Chocolate tabby point

- The body is ivory. The points are milk chocolate tabby, except for gloves that are white.
- Nose leather is pale red, pink, or milk chocolate.

Chocolate tortie point

- The body is ivory. The points are milk chocolate patched or mingled with red and/or light red, except for gloves that are white.
- Nose leather is milk chocolate and/or pink.

Chocolate torbie point

- The body is ivory. The points have tabby markings in milk chocolate patched or mingled with red and/or light red, except for gloves that are white.
- Nose leather is milk chocolate, light red, or pink, or milk chocolate mottled with light red and/or pink.

Blue tortie point

- The body is bluish white. The points are blue gray patched or mottled with pastel cream, except for gloves that are white.
- Nose leather is blue gray and/or pink.

Blue torbie point

- The body is glacial white with a slight bluish tinge. The points have tabby markings in blue gray patched or mingled with pastel cream, except for gloves that are white.
- Nose leather is blue gray, old rose, or pink, or blue gray mottled with old rose and/or pink.

Red tabby point

- The body is off-white with a slight red tinge, known as a halo. The points are warm orange tabby, except for gloves that are white.
- Nose leather is pink or brick red.

Cream tabby point

- The body is off-white. The points are cream tabby, except for gloves that are white.
- Nose leather is pink.

Lilac tabby point

- The body is glacial white with lilac tabby points, except for gloves that are white.
- Nose leather is pink or lavender pink.

Lilac tortie point

- The body is glacial white. The points are lilac patched or mingled with pale cream, except for gloves that are white.
- Nose leather is lavender pink and/or pink.

Lilac torbie point

- The body is glacial white. The points have tabby markings in lilac patched or mingled with pale cream, except for gloves that are white.
- Nose leather is lavender pink or pale pink, or lavender pink mottled with pale pink.

Semi-longhaired Breeds

Maine Coon

One of the oldest of the natural breeds of North America, the Maine Coon has been known as a true variety for over a hundred years. Originating in Maine, it was thought to be a cross between semi-wild domestic cats and raccoons, now known to be biologically impossible. Another legend tells how Marie Antoinette, in planning her escape from the horrors of the French Revolution, sent her cats to be cared for in Maine until she could find a new home. Today's more enlightened view is that long-coated cats such as the Angora may have been introduced to coastal towns by seamen, and these bred with domestic cats resulting eventually in the large and handsome American longhaired breed of today.

A tabby version of the Maine Coon is recorded as having won the Best in Show award at the Madison Square Garden Cat Show in 1895, but with the introduction of more striking breeds from Europe at the turn of the century, the popularity of

RED SHADED MAINE COON
In shaded varieties, the basic color should be deepest on the head, back, and paws.

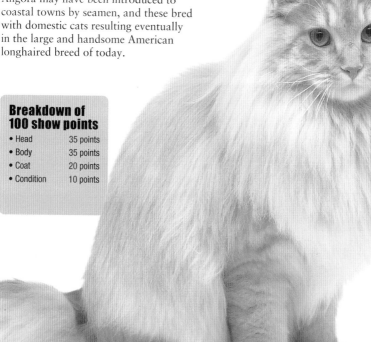

Breakdown of 100 show points
- Head   35 points
- Body   35 points
- Coat   20 points
- Condition   10 points

Category Longhair.

Overall build Medium to large. Males are usually larger than females.

Body Long with substantial bone, large framed and well proportioned, muscular, and broad chested.

Colors Recognized in all colors except the Himalayan and Burmese patterns, and chocolate, cinnamon, lilac, or fawn. There is no relationship between coat and eye color, though brilliant eye color is desirable. Any amount of white is allowed.

Tail At least as long as the body from shoulder blade to base of the tail; wide at the base tapering to the tip, with full, flowing hair.

Head Medium size with a squarish outline; gently concave in profile, with curved forehead and prominent cheekbones.

Ears Large, wide at the base, moderately pointed with lynx-like ear tufts, set high but well apart.

Coat Heavy with a silky texture. Short on the head, shoulders, and legs, becoming longer down the back and sides, shaggy on the hind legs and belly. Full ruff.

Eyes Large, slightly oval, but not almond shaped, and set slanted toward the outer base of the ear.

Nose Medium length.

Chin Firm and in vertical alignment with the nose and upper lip.

Legs Medium length.

Paws Large, round, and tufted between the toes.

Penalties given for

- Short or uneven coat
- Lack of undercoat
- Unbalanced proportions
- Delicate bone structure
- Long, thin legs
- Short tail
- Wide-set or flared ears
- Pronounced whisker pads
- Straight or convex profile
- Slanted, almond-shaped eyes

the Maine Coon declined. Though the breed flourished as a popular and hardy pet for some years, it was not until 1953 that the Central Maine Coon Cat Club was formed to promote the breed. By 1967 a show standard was accepted by American cat associations. In 1976 the International Society for the Preservation of the Maine Coon was formed, and the Cat Fanciers' Association accepted the breed with full championship status.

Character and care

Considered by their fans to be the perfect domestic pets, typical Maine Coons are extrovert, playful, and amusing. Their coat is long and flowing but rarely gets matted, and is easy to care for by combing through occasionally.

Maine Coon: SOLID & PARTICOLOR VARIETIES

The standard for solid colors insists on a coat that is sound and free from any shading, markings, or hair of another color. Tortoiseshell varieties have clearly defined and well-broken patches of color.

White

- The coat is pure, glistening white with no markings.
- Nose leather and paw pads are pink; eye color is blue, orange, odd, or green. The Maine Coon White is one of the few pedigree breeds in which the white variety may have green eyes.

Black

- The coat is dense, coal black, sound from the roots to the tips of the hair, with no sign of rustiness on the tips and no smoke undercoat.
- Nose leather is black; paw pads are black or brown.

Red

- The coat is deep, clear, rich brilliant red without shading, markings, or ticking.
- Lips and chin are the same color as the coat. Nose leather and paw pads are brick red.

Blue

- The coat is an even tone of gray blue from the nose to tail tip, and must be sound to the roots.
- Nose leather and paw pads are blue.

Dilute calico

- The coat is the same as the blue-cream, except here there must be white on the bib, belly, and all four paws.
- Feet must be white with no trace of blue or cream, and an area of white on the face is desirable. Nose leather and paw pads are rose.

Cream

- The coat is an even shade of buff cream, without any markings, and must be sound to the roots.
- Nose leather and paw pads are pink.

Bicolor

- This is a combination of a solid color with white. The accepted colors are black, blue, red, and cream.
- The colored areas of hair predominate, with white areas on the face, chest, belly, legs, and feet.

Tortoiseshell

- The coat is black with unbrindled patches of red and light red, clearly defined and well broken.
- A blaze of red or light red on the face is desirable.

Blue-cream

- The coat is blue with clearly defined, unbrindled, well-broken patches of cream on the body and extremities.
- This is a dilute form of tortoiseshell, and so is usually female, with males being very rare.

Calico

- The coat is pale red and dense black, and there must be white on the bib, belly, and all four paws. White on a third of the body overall is desirable.
- Nose leather and paw pads are black; eye color is usually deep orange.

Maine Coon: SMOKE & SHADED VARIETIES

*Any solid or tortie color is accepted.
The base coat should be as white as possible,
with the tips of the hairs shaded the varietal
color, darkest on the head, back, and paws.*

Shaded silver
- The white undercoat is tipped with black, graduating to white on the chin, chest, stomach, and underside of the tail. The legs are the same tone as the face.
- Eye rims, lips, and nose are outlined with black; nose leather is brick red; paw pads are black.

Black smoke
- The white undercoat is deeply tipped with black. The points and mask are black, with a narrow band of white at the base of the hairs next to the skin.
- Ruff and ear tufts are light silver; nose leather and paw pads are black.

Blue smoke
- The white undercoat is deeply tipped with blue. The points and mask are blue, with a narrow band of white at the base of the hairs next to the skin.
- Ruff and ear tufts are white; nose leather and paw pads are blue.

Red smoke
- The white undercoat is deeply tipped with red. The points and mask are red, with a narrow band of white at the base of the hairs next to the skin.
- Eye rims, nose leather, and paw pads are rose.

Red shaded
- The white undercoat is tipped with red, graduating to white on the chin, chest, stomach, and underside of the tail. The legs are the same tone as the face.
- Nose leather and paw pads are black.

Cream smoke
- This is a dilute version of the red smoke in which the red tipping is reduced to pale cream.
- Eye rims, nose leather, and paw pads are rose.

Maine Coon: TABBY VARIETIES

*Both classic tabby and mackerel tabby patterned cats
are accepted in any of the following colors.*

Silver tabby

- The coat is pale, clear silver with dense black markings. White is allowed around the lips.
- Nose leather is brick red; paw pads are black.

Blue tabby

- The coat is pale bluish ivory with very deep blue markings that afford a good contrast with the base color. There is a warm fawn patina over the whole coat. White is allowed around the lips and chin.
- Nose leather is old rose; paw pads are rose.

Red tabby

- The coat is vibrant red with deep, rich red markings. White is allowed around the lips and chin.
- Nose leather and paw pads are brick red; green or brown eyes are the most common.

Cream tabby

- The coat is very pale cream with buff or cream markings that are sufficiently dark to afford a good contrast with the base color. White is allowed around the lips and chin.
- Nose leather and paw pads are pink.

Cameo tabby

- The coat is off-white with red markings. White is allowed around the lips and chin.
- Nose leather and paw pads are rose.

Maine Coon: TABBY VARIETIES *continued*

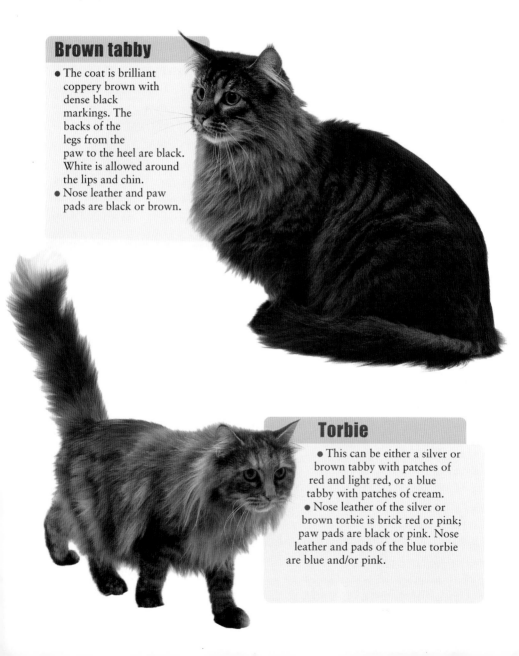

Brown tabby

- The coat is brilliant coppery brown with dense black markings. The backs of the legs from the paw to the heel are black. White is allowed around the lips and chin.
- Nose leather and paw pads are black or brown.

Torbie

- This can be either a silver or brown tabby with patches of red and light red, or a blue tabby with patches of cream.
- Nose leather of the silver or brown torbie is brick red or pink; paw pads are black or pink. Nose leather and pads of the blue torbie are blue and/or pink.

Tabby and white

- The cat may be any tabby color—silver, brown, blue, red, or cream—with or without white on the face, but with white on the bib, belly, and all four paws. White on a third of the body overall is desirable.
- Nose leather and paw pads as for the torbie.

Torbie and white

- The main coloring is as described for the torbie, but with white markings as defined for the tabby and white. Colors accepted are silver, brown, and blue.
- Nose leather is the main varietal color; paw pads are usually pink.

Ragdoll

The first Ragdoll cats were bred by an American, Ann Baker, whose white longhaired cat Josephine was involved in a road accident that left her with permanent injuries. When Josephine eventually had kittens, they were found to have particularly placid temperaments and would completely relax when picked up and cuddled, reminiscent of a ragdoll.

The name was chosen and recognized in 1965 by the National Cat Fanciers' Association, and later by other associations. Although this breed's alleged inability to feel pain or fear, or to fight with other animals, is claimed to be due to Josephine's accident, this goes against all genetic reasoning. The specialized temperament is almost certainly due to the fact that only cats of a loving disposition were selected in the first matings. The three patterns found in the breed could certainly have been produced by Josephine if the stud cat

Breakdown of 100 show points

• Head	20 points
• Body & neck	20 points
• Color & markings	20 points
• Coat	10 points
• Eyes	10 points
• Legs & paws	10 points
• Ears	5 points
• Tail	5 points

BLUE POINT MITTED RAGDOLL
In the mitted pattern of the Ragdoll breed, the four paws are white to the same degree as that found in the Birman.

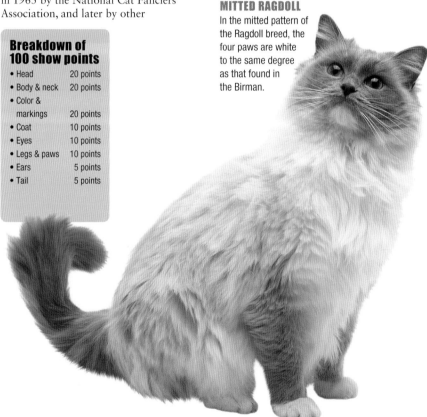

Key characteristics

Category Longhair.

Overall build Large.

Body Long, with medium bone structure, muscular, broad chest, and muscular hindquarters.

Colors Colorpoint, mitted, and bicolor in seal, blue, chocolate, and lilac, all with clear blue eyes.

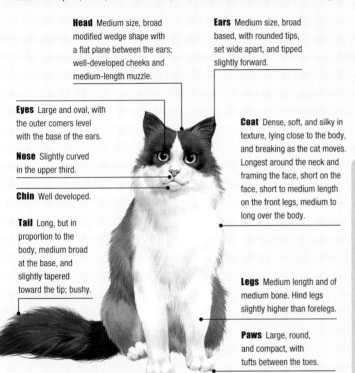

Head Medium size, broad modified wedge shape with a flat plane between the ears; well-developed cheeks and medium-length muzzle.

Ears Medium size, broad based, with rounded tips, set wide apart, and tipped slightly forward.

Eyes Large and oval, with the outer corners level with the base of the ears.

Nose Slightly curved in the upper third.

Chin Well developed.

Tail Long, but in proportion to the body, medium broad at the base, and slightly tapered toward the tip; bushy.

Coat Dense, soft, and silky in texture, lying close to the body, and breaking as the cat moves. Longest around the neck and framing the face, short on the face, short to medium length on the front legs, medium to long over the body.

Legs Medium length and of medium bone. Hind legs slightly higher than forelegs.

Paws Large, round, and compact, with tufts between the toes.

Penalties given for

- Narrow head
- Roman nose
- Too large a stop in profile
- Too small or pointed ears
- Almond-shaped eyes
- Too long or too thin neck
- Cobby body
- Narrow chest
- Short legs
- Splayed feet
- Lack of toe tufts
- Short or blunt-tipped tail
- Eye color other than blue

used had carried genes for the Himalayan pattern and long coat, and if either Josephine or her mate had also carried the gene for white spotting.

Though some controversy remains over the breed, the Ragdoll has gained popularity around the world, and it has become an interesting addition to the show scene.

Character and care

The Ragdoll is an exceptionally affectionate, loving, and relaxed cat. Although it is generally calm and placid, with a quiet voice, it loves to play and to be petted. The thick coat does not form mats and is therefore quite easy to groom with regular gentle brushing of the body and combing through the longer hair on the tail and around the neck.

Ragdoll: COLORPOINT VARIETIES

The body is light in color and only slightly shaded.
The points—ears, mask, legs, and tail—should be
clearly defined, and matched for color and in harmony
with the body color. No white hairs are allowed.

Seal point

- The body is pale fawn or cream.
- The points are deep seal brown, except for the white areas.

Chocolate point

- The body is ivory.
- The points are milk chocolate, except for the white areas.

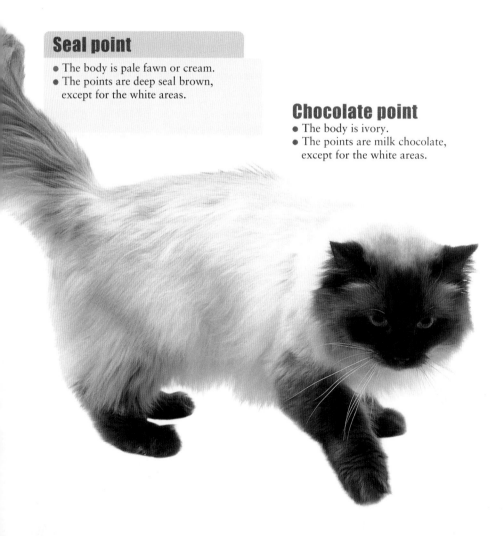

Blue point

- The body is cold-toned bluish white.
- The points are blue, except for the white areas.

Lilac point

- The body is glacial white.
- The points are frosty gray of a pinkish tone, except for the white areas.

Ragdoll: MITTED VARIETIES

The mitted variety is the same as the colorpoint but with white front paws. The back paws should be entirely white to the knees and hocks.

Seal point

- As with all mitted Ragdolls, the chin must be white, and a white stripe on the nose is preferred. A white stripe extends from the bib between the front legs to the base of the tail.
- The body is pale fawn or cream. The points are deep seal brown, except for the white areas.

Blue point

- The body is cold-toned bluish white.
- The points are blue, except for the white areas.

Chocolate point

- The body is ivory.
- The points are milk chocolate, except for the white areas.

Lilac point

- The body is glacial white.
- The points are frosty gray of a pinkish tone, except for the white areas.

Ragdoll: BICOLOR VARIETIES

The body is light in color. The points—ears, mask, and tail—should be well defined. The mask has an inverted white "V," the stomach is white, and the legs are preferably white. No white is allowed on the ears or tail.

Seal point

- The body is pale fawn or cream.
- The points are deep seal brown, except for the white areas.

Chocolate point

- The body is ivory.
- The points are milk chocolate, except for the white areas.

Blue point

- The body is cold-toned bluish-white.
- The points are blue, except for the white areas.

Lilac point

- The body is glacial white.
- The points are frosty gray of a pinkish tone, except for the white areas.

Norwegian Forest Cat

Known as the Norsk Skaukatt in its native Norway, the Norwegian Forest Cat is very similar to the Maine Coon in many ways. It is a uniquely Scandinavian breed whose origins are shrouded in mystery, and it is referred to in Norse myths and mid-nineteenth-century fairy stories. Having evolved naturally in the cold climate of Norway, it has a heavy, weather-resistant coat. The glossy, medium-length top coat hangs from the spine line, keeping out rain and snow, while the woolly undercoat keeps the body comfortably warm. Its strong legs, paws, and claws make the Forest Cat an extremely good climber in trees and on rocky slopes. It is highly intelligent, nimble, and an excellent hunter.

From these naturally evolved cats, a group of breeders set out in the 1930s to develop a pedigree breed, starting with

Breakdown of 100 show points

- Body — 25 points
- Coat — 25 points
- Head — 20 points
- Ears — 10 points
- Tail — 10 points
- Eye shape — 5 points
- Condition — 5 points

RED SILVER TABBY AND WHITE NORWEGIAN FOREST CAT
The addition of silver to other varieties adds to the range of pale, attractive shades.

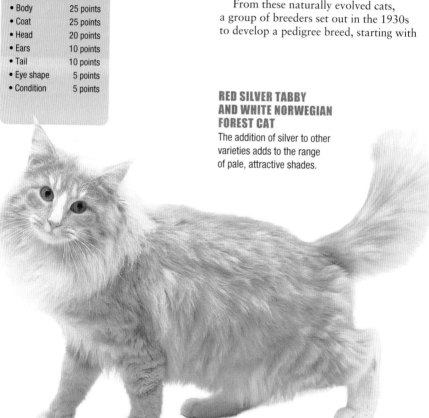

Key characteristics

Category Longhair.

Overall build Large.

Body Long, strongly built, with solid bone structure.

Colors All colors except chocolate, cinnamon, lilac, and fawn are accepted, though neither the Himalayan pattern nor the Burmese factor is allowed. Type always takes preference over color. There is no relationship between coat and eye color, but clear eye color is desirable.

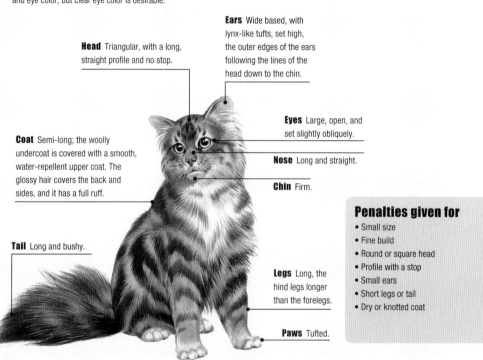

Head Triangular, with a long, straight profile and no stop.

Ears Wide based, with lynx-like tufts, set high, the outer edges of the ears following the lines of the head down to the chin.

Eyes Large, open, and set slightly obliquely.

Nose Long and straight.

Chin Firm.

Coat Semi-long; the woolly undercoat is covered with a smooth, water-repellent upper coat. The glossy hair covers the back and sides, and it has a full ruff.

Tail Long and bushy.

Legs Long, the hind legs longer than the forelegs.

Paws Tufted.

Penalties given for

- Small size
- Fine build
- Round or square head
- Profile with a stop
- Small ears
- Short legs or tail
- Dry or knotted coat

some hardy farm cats. As a breed, the Forest Cat gained in popularity during the 1970s and was granted full championship status in FIFe in 1977.

The ideal show cat differs from the Maine Coon in having hind legs longer than the forelegs, and the standard of points specifies a double coat, which is permitted but not desirable in the American breed.

Character and care

Strong and hardy, the Forest Cat can be very playful while retaining the strongly independent character of its semi-wild ancestors. It enjoys human company and can be very affectionate, but dislikes too much cosseting. The trouble-free coat periodically needs combing through to keep the undercoat in good condition and to clean the flowing tail and full ruff.

Norwegian Forest Cat: SOLID VARIETIES

The coat should be sound in color and free from any shading, markings, or color other than the varietal one. Any eye color is allowed.

White

- The coat is pure, glistening white.
- Nose leather and paw pads are pink.

Black

- The coat is dense, coal black, sound from the roots to the tips of the hair, with no sign of rustiness on the tips, and no smoke undercoat.
- Nose leather is black; paw pads are black or brown.

Blue

- The coat is an even tone of gray blue from nose to tail tip, and must be sound to the roots.
- Nose leather and paw pads are blue.

Red

- The coat is deep, clear, rich, brilliant red without any shading, markings, or ticking. The lips and chin must be the same color as the coat.
- Nose leather and paw pads are brick red.

Cream

- The coat is an even shade of buff cream, without any markings, and must be sound to the roots.
- Nose leather and paw pads are pink.

Norwegian Forest Cat: TABBY VARIETIES

Any of the four tabby patterns are accepted and a range of colors except the chocolate and lilac series. Any amount of white on the body is also permitted.

Brown tabby

- The coat is brilliant coppery brown with dense black markings. The backs of the legs from paw to heel are black; white is allowed around the lips and chin.
- Nose leather and paw pads are black or brown.

Red tabby

- The coat is red with deep, rich red markings; white is allowed around the lips and chin.
- Nose leather and paw pads are brick red.

Cream tabby

- The coat is very pale cream with buff or cream markings sufficiently darker to afford a good contrast with the base color. White is allowed around the lips and chin.
- Nose leather and paw pads are pink.

Tabby and white

- This variety may be silver, brown, blue, red, or cream, with or without white on the face, but with white on the bib, belly, and all four paws. White on a third of the body overall is desirable.
- Nose leather and paw pads are as for appropriate the tabby color.

Silver tabby

- The coat is pale, clear silver with dense black markings; white is allowed around the lips and chin.
- Nose leather is brick red; paw pads are black.

Blue tabby

- The coat is pale bluish ivory with very deep blue markings affording a good contrast with the base color. There is a warm fawn patina over the whole coat. White is allowed around the lips and chin.
- Nose leather is old rose; paw pads are rose.

Norwegian Forest Cat:
PARTICOLOR VARIETIES

A wide range of coat colors and patterns is acceptable. Unlike most other pedigree breeds, there is no relationship between coat color and eye color.

Bicolor

- The accepted colors are black, blue, red, and cream.
- The varietal color should predominate, with white areas located on the face, chest, belly, legs, and feet.

Tortoiseshell

- The coat is black with unbrindled patches of red and light red; the patches should be clearly defined and well broken on the body and extremities. A blaze of red on the face is desirable.
- All colors of torties are accepted and may be with or without white markings.

Calico

- The color is as for the tortoiseshell, with or without white on the face, but there must be white on the bib, belly, and all four paws.
- White on a third of the body overall is desirable.

Blue-cream

- The coat is blue with clearly defined, unbrindled, well-broken patches of cream on the body and extremities.

Dilute calico

- The color is as defined for the blue-cream, with or without white on the face, but there must be white on the bib, belly, and all four paws.
- White on a third of the body overall is desirable.

Norwegian Forest Cat:
SMOKE & CAMEO VARIETIES

The long coat is particularly attractive in the colors that have a silver undercoat, such as the smoke, shaded, tipped, and cameo series.

Smoke

- The coat is white deeply tipped with black, blue, or red. The points and mask are black, blue, or red, respectively, with a narrow band of white at the base of the hairs next to the skin.
- Nose leather and paw pads are black, blue, or rose.

Chinchilla silver

- The coat is pure white tipped with black on the back, flanks, head, and tail. The legs may be slightly shaded with tipping. The chin, ear tufts, stomach, and chest are pure white.
- Eye rims, lips, and nose are outlined with black; nose leather and paw pads are black.

Shaded silver

- The coat is white with a mantle of black tipping, graduating from dark on the spine to white on the chin, chest, stomach, and underside of the tail. The legs are the same tone as the face.
- Eye rims, lips, and nose are outlined with black; nose leather is brick red; paw pads are black.

Red shell cameo

- The coat is white tipped with red on the back, flanks, head, and tail. The face and legs may be slightly shaded with tipping. The chin, ear tufts, stomach, and chest are white.
- Eye rims, nose leather, and paw pads are rose.

Red shaded cameo

- The coat is white with a mantle of red tipping, graduating from dark on the spine to white on the chin, chest, stomach, and underside of the tail. The legs are the same tone as the face.
- Nose leather and paw pads are black.

Turkish Angora

One of the most ancient of cat breeds, originating in Turkey, the Angora was the first of the longhaired cats to reach Europe. In the sixteenth century, a naturalist called Nicholas-Claude Fabri de Peiresc imported several cats into France from Angora (now Ankara) in Turkey. They were described in contemporary literature as "ash-colored dun and speckled cats, beautiful to behold." The cats were bred from, and some of the kittens went to England, where they were highly prized and known as French cats. When another type of long-coated cat arrived in Europe from Persia (now Iran), the Angora and the Persian were intermated quite indiscriminately.

The Persian type gradually superseded the Angora type in popularity, and by the twentieth century the Angora breed was virtually unknown outside its native land.

During the 1950s and 1960s, North America, Britain, and Sweden imported cats from Turkey to start breeding programs for the development of the Angora breed. In the United States, the

Breakdown of 100 show points

• Coat	40 points
• Head & neck	15 points
• Body	15 points
• Eye color	10 points
• Eye shape & settings	5 points
• Ears	5 points
• Tail	5 points
• Legs & paws	5 points

LILAC ANGORA
This is an excellent example of the variety, showing very good type and a true lilac coat—frosty gray with a pinkish tone.

Key characteristics

Category Longhair.

Overall build Medium, with males larger than females.

Body Fine boned, with a light-framed chest and slender torso. Lithe, with the hind part higher than the front.

Colors White with amber, blue, or odd eyes; black, blue, chocolate, red, cream, cinnamon, caramel, fawn; silver and non-silver tabby in any pattern and all colors; bicolor, tortie, blue-cream, calico, dilute calico, torbie, smoke, shaded.

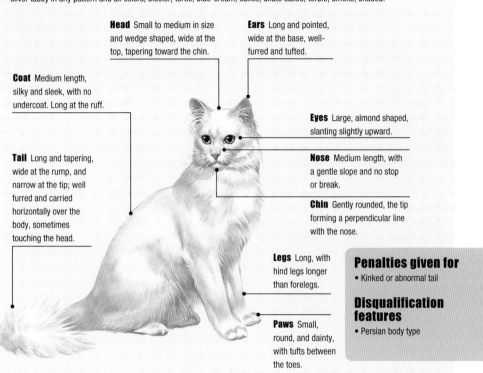

Head Small to medium in size and wedge shaped, wide at the top, tapering toward the chin.

Ears Long and pointed, wide at the base, well-furred and tufted.

Coat Medium length, silky and sleek, with no undercoat. Long at the ruff.

Eyes Large, almond shaped, slanting slightly upward.

Tail Long and tapering, wide at the rump, and narrow at the tip; well furred and carried horizontally over the body, sometimes touching the head.

Nose Medium length, with a gentle slope and no stop or break.

Chin Gently rounded, the tip forming a perpendicular line with the nose.

Legs Long, with hind legs longer than forelegs.

Paws Small, round, and dainty, with tufts between the toes.

Penalties given for
• Kinked or abnormal tail

Disqualification features
• Persian body type

Turkish Angora was officially recognized and granted championship status by some associations in the early 1970s, but until 1978, the CFA only accepted the white variety. Eventually, however, a wide range of colors was accepted.

Character and care
Precocious as kittens, Angoras are playful and athletic. They are generally affectionate with their owners, but can be aloof with strangers.

Angoras molt excessively in the summer, and the loose hair should be combed out daily. The lack of a fluffy undercoat means that the coat does not become matted.

Turkish Angora: SOLID & OTHER VARIETIES

In the UK, the Angora has been granted preliminary show status as the long-coated equivalent of the Javanese.

White
- The coat is pure white with no other coloring.
- Nose leather and paw pads are pink; eye color is amber, blue, or odd (one blue, one amber).

Blue
- The coat is an even tone of blue from nose to tail tip with the color sound to the roots. Denser shades of blue are preferred.
- Nose leather and paw pads are blue; eye color is amber.

Red
- The coat is deep, rich, clear, brilliant red without shading, markings, or ticking. The lips and chin should be the same color as the coat.
- Nose leather and paw pads are brick red; the eye color is amber.

Cream
- The coat is an even shade of buff cream without markings, and with the color sound to the roots. Lighter shades are preferred.
- Nose leather and paw pads are pink; eye color is amber.

Blue-cream
- The coat is predominantly blue with patches of solid cream. The patches should be clearly defined and well broken on both the body and extremities.
- Eye color is amber.

Black

- The coat is dense coal black, sound from the roots to the tips of the hair, and free from any tinge of rust on the tips, or a smoke undercoat.
- Nose leather is black; paw pads are black or brown; eye color is amber.

Tortoiseshell

- The coat is black with unbrindled and clearly defined patches of red and light red. A blaze of red or light red on the face is desirable.
- Eye color is amber.

Calico

- The coat is white with unbrindled patches of black and red; white is predominant on the underparts.
- Eye color is amber.

Dilute calico

- The coat is white with unbrindled patches of blue and cream; white is predominant on the underparts.
- Eye color is amber.

Bicolor

- Varieties are black and white, blue and white, red and white, or cream and white. The muzzle, chest, legs, feet, and underparts should be white in each. White under the tail and a white collar are permissible. An inverted V-shaped blaze on the face is desirable.
- Eye color is amber.

Smoke

- The coat is white deeply tipped with black or blue. The mask and points are black or blue with a narrow band of white at the base of the hairs next to the skin.
- Nose leather and paw pads are black in the black smoke or blue in the blue smoke; eye color is amber in both.

Tabby

- Classic and mackerel tabby patterns are accepted in silver, brown, blue, and red.
- Nose leather is brick red in the silver, brown, and red tabby; or old rose in the blue tabby. Paw pads are black in the silver tabby; black or brown in the brown tabby; rose in the blue tabby; or brick red in the red tabby. Eye color is green or hazel in the silver tabby; or amber in the brown, blue, and red tabby.

Turkish Van

The cat known as the Turkish in Britain and the Turkish Van in Europe and the United States was first introduced to Britain and the cat fanciers of the world in 1955 by Laura Lushington. Traveling in the lake Van district of Turkey, she and a friend were enchanted by these cats and eventually acquired the first breeding pair. Others of the breed were imported into Britain, and the necessary breeding programs were completed in order to apply for official recognition of the cats as a pure breed in their own right. This was achieved in 1969, and the cats attracted considerable attention.

Turkish Van cats were also introduced independently from Turkey directly to the United States, where they are now recognized by some associations.

Breakdown of 100 show points

• Head	25 points
• Body	25 points
• Coat	25 points
• Eye color	10 points
• Ears	10 points
• Condition	5 points

AUBURN TURKISH VAN
The markings of the Turkish Van are responsible for the "van" designation in other varieties that are mostly white, with small and discrete areas of color.

Category Longhair.
Overall build Medium and heavy.
Body Long but sturdy and muscular.
Colors Auburn: chalk white coat with no trace of yellow; auburn markings on face with a white blaze; auburn tail; white ears; eye rims, nose leather, paw pads, and inside ears are shell pink; eye color is amber, blue, or odd.
Cream: chalk white coat with no trace of yellow; cream markings on face with a white blaze; cream tail; white ears; eye rims, nose leather, paw pads, and inside ears are shell pink; eye color is amber, blue, or odd.

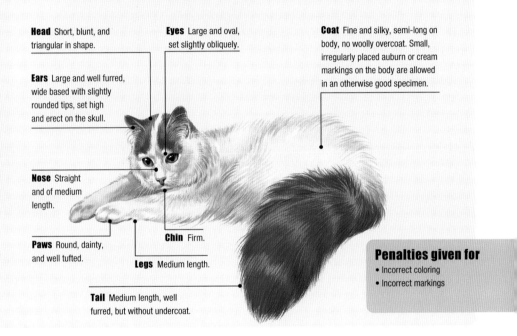

Head Short, blunt, and triangular in shape.

Eyes Large and oval, set slightly obliquely.

Coat Fine and silky, semi-long on body, no woolly overcoat. Small, irregularly placed auburn or cream markings on the body are allowed in an otherwise good specimen.

Ears Large and well furred, wide based with slightly rounded tips, set high and erect on the skull.

Nose Straight and of medium length.

Paws Round, dainty, and well tufted.

Chin Firm.

Legs Medium length.

Tail Medium length, well furred, but without undercoat.

Penalties given for
- Incorrect coloring
- Incorrect markings

Character and care

The first cats imported from Turkey were inclined to be slightly nervous of human contact, but today's Turkish cats generally have affectionate dispositions. They are strong and hardy, and breeders were intrigued by the animals' natural liking for water—they will voluntarily swim if given the opportunity and have no objection to being bathed in preparation for show appearances.

The silky coat has no woolly undercoat, making grooming an easy task.

Shorthaired Breeds

British Shorthair

This breed probably evolved from domestic cats introduced to the British Isles by Roman colonists some 2,000 years ago. Shorthairs appeared in substantial numbers in the first cat shows held toward the end of the nineteenth century, then seemed to lose their popularity in favor of Persian and Angora cats. It was not until the 1930s that a general resurgence of the breed began.

British Shorthairs suffered a setback during World War II, when many owners had to give up breeding pedigree kittens and neutered their cats. In the post-war years, very few pedigree stud males remained, and the Shorthair's type suffered after outcrosses were made with shorthaired cats of foreign type. Matters were redressed during the early 1950s by careful matings with blue Persians, and within a few generations the British Shorthair was brought up to the exacting standards existing today. In the United States, as in the UK, British Shorthairs are bred only to other British Shorthairs, and backcrossing to Persians is no longer allowed.

Breakdown of 100 show points

- Coat   35 points
- Body, legs,
     & paws   25 points
- Head & ears   20 points
- Eyes   10 points
- Tail   10 points

BLUE TABBY BRITISH SHORTHAIR
In dilute varieties like this blue tabby, the pattern is soft and diffused.

Category Shorthair.

Overall build Large and chunky, but not coarse or overweight.

Body Powerful, with a level back and broad chest.

Colors White, black, blue, cream, blue-cream, lilac, chocolate, bicolor (all colors), tortoiseshell, lilac tortie, chocolate tortie, calico, dilute calico, tabby (classic, mackerel, and spotted: all colors), torbie (all colors), smoke (all colors), tipped (all colors), colorpoint (all colors).

Head Very broad and round with well-developed cheeks, set on a short, thick neck.

Ears Medium size, broad based, round tipped, and set far apart.

Tail Length in proportion to body, thick at the base, and tapering to a rounded tip.

Coat Short and dense, not double or woolly. Firm and resilient to the touch.

Eyes Large, round, and well opened.

Nose Medium broad with gentle dip in profile.

Chin Firm and well developed.

Legs Short to medium length and well boned.

Paws Round.

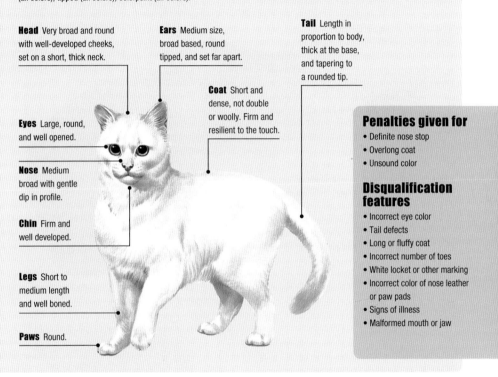

Penalties given for

- Definite nose stop
- Overlong coat
- Unsound color

Disqualification features

- Incorrect eye color
- Tail defects
- Long or fluffy coat
- Incorrect number of toes
- White locket or other marking
- Incorrect color of nose leather or paw pads
- Signs of illness
- Malformed mouth or jaw

Character and care

The typical British Shorthair has a sweet and gentle nature and makes an undemanding, quiet-voiced pet. It is generally calm and intelligent, and readily responds to affection.

Although it has a short coat, this is quite dense and needs regular grooming by brushing and combing right through to the roots every day. It is particularly important to accustom all kittens to this daily procedure from a very early age so that it is not resented later. The eyes and ears should be gently cleaned with a cotton swab whenever necessary, and the coat may be polished with a grooming mitt or a silk scarf.

British Shorthair: SOLID VARIETIES

The most popular of the British Shorthairs is the blue, with its round, glowing eyes. The black and white British Shorthairs have coats more difficult to produce to top show standard.

Black

- The coat is shining jet black to the roots, with no rusty tinge. There must be no white hairs anywhere.
- Nose leather is black; paw pads are black or brown; eye color is gold, orange, or copper with no trace of green.

White

- The coat is pure white with no sign of yellow tingeing. The nose leather and paw pads are pink.
- The blue-eyed white has eyes of a deep sapphire blue and is penalized for green rims or flecks in the eye. The orange-eyed white has deep orange, gold, or copper eyes.

Cream

- The coat is rich, light cream and should be as free from tabby markings as possible. There must be no white markings anywhere, and the cream color should be sound to the roots.
- Nose leather and paw pads are pink; eye color is orange, copper, or gold.

Blue

- The coat should be very even in color and of a light to medium blue tone, lighter shades being preferred. No tabby or white markings are allowed anywhere.
- Nose leather and paw pads are blue; eye color is gold, orange, or copper.

British Shorthair: SOLID VARIETIES

continued

Blue-cream

- In the US, the coat should be distinctly blue with cream patches; in the UK, the coat should be evenly intermingled blue gray and pale cream.
- Nose leather and paw pads are blue and/or pink; eye color is gold, orange, or copper.

Lilac

- A comparatively recent addition to the British Shorthair color list, the lilac conforms to the usual standard for conformation.
- It has an even-colored, frosty gray coat with a distinctly pinkish cast.

British Shorthair: BICOLOR VARIETIES

Bicolor Shorthairs are cats of just two colors: a standard color with white. It is important for the markings to be as symmetrical as possible to present a balanced impression.

CREAM & WHITE BICOLOR
Symmetry of coloring is desired in the British bicolor, with not more than half of the cat to be white.

BLUE & WHITE BICOLOR
This cat is very evenly marked, with a good shade of medium blue in the basic coat color.

Bicolor

- Bicolors may be any of the main varietal colors with white. There must be no tabby markings in the solid-colored areas.
- Nose leather and paw pads are generally pink; eye color is gold, orange, or copper.

British Shorthair:
TORTOISESHELL VARIETIES

British tortoiseshells are penalized for brindling, tabby markings, unequal balance of color or markings, and unbroken color on the paws.

Tortoiseshell

- The coat should have brilliant black and red markings, both dark and light, equally balanced over the head, body, legs, and tail. A red blaze down the face is desirable.
- Nose leather and paw pads are pink and/or black; eye color is gold, orange, or copper (hazel is also allowed by some associations).

LILAC TORTIE
An admixture of lilac and pale cream produces a pastel effect over the body.

CHOCOLATE TORTIE
Warm chocolate mixed with red and light red make up the bright coloring of the coat.

Calico

- The coat should be equally balanced in black and red, both light and dark, on white. There should be a white blaze down the face.
- Nose leather and paws are pink and/or black; eye color is gold, orange, or copper (hazel is also allowed by some associations).

Dilute calico

- The coat is patched with bold areas of blue and cream highlighted by white markings.
  - Nose leather and paws are pink and/or black; eye color is gold, orange, or copper (hazel is also allowed by some associations).

British Shorthair: TABBY VARIETIES

*Classic, mackerel, and spotted tabby patterns
are accepted in a wide variety of colors.*

Brown tabby

- The coat is rich sable or brown with dense black markings. The lips and chin are the same as the rings around the eyes. The backs of the legs are black from heel to paw.
- Nose leather is brick red; paw pads are black or brown; eye color is gold, orange, or copper (some associations allow green or hazel).

Silver tabby

- The coat, including lips and chin, is pale clear silver with dense black markings.
- Nose leather is brick red; paw pads are black; eye color is green or hazel.

Cream tabby

- The coat, including lips and chin, is very pale cream with buff or cream markings that are dark enough to contrast well with the ground color.
- Nose leather and paw pads are pink; eye color is gold or copper.

Red tabby

- The coat, including lips and chin, is red with deep, rich red markings.
- Nose leather and paw pads are brick red; eye color is gold, orange, or copper (some associations accept hazel).

Blue tabby

- The coat, including lips and chin, is pale bluish ivory with very deep blue markings. There should be an overall warm fawn patina.
  - Nose leather is old rose; paw pads are rose; eye color is gold or copper.

Torbie

- The tabby pattern is patched with red, light red, or cream, depending on the main varietal color (red or light red on non-dilute color varieties; cream on dilute color varieties).
- Nose leather, paw pads, and eyes are as for the varietal color.

British Shorthair: OTHER VARIETIES

*Other varieties of the British Shorthair include
the tipped, smoke, and colorpoint.*

Tipped

- The coat can be tipped in any recognizable color.
- A genetically silver variety, the color is restricted to the very tips of the hairs of the coat, while the undercoat is so pale that it appears to be pure white.

Black smoke

- The coat is white or silver deeply tipped with black.
- Nose leather and paw pads are black; eye color is gold or copper.

Blue smoke

- The coat is white or silver deeply tipped with blue.
- Nose leather and paw pads are blue; eye color is gold or copper.

Colorpoint

- A range of points colors is accepted. Any shading on the body should be of the same tone as the points.
- Although the standard requires eye color in the colorpoint to be a clear, definite blue, this has proved difficult to achieve in most varieties.

RED COLORPOINT
The mask, ears, legs, and tail should be clearly defined and well matched.

LILAC-CREAM COLORPOINT
This is a very ethereal color, the points being delicately mingled shades of palest lilac and cream.

CREAM COLORPOINT
There should be good contrast between the points and the body color.

Chartreux

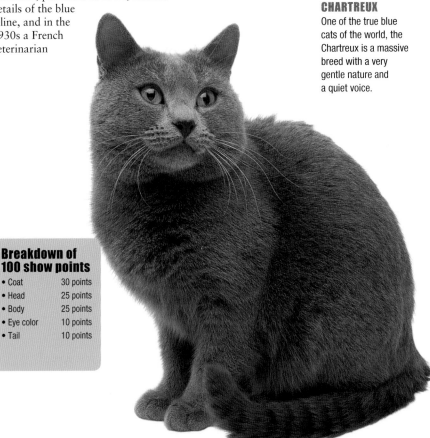

Native to France, the Chartreux is said to have been bred exclusively by Carthusian monks as long ago as the sixteenth century. The monks lived in the monastery near the town of Grenoble, world famous for its unique liqueur, known as Chartreuse. The naturalist Georges Louis Buffon's work *Histoire Naturelle*, published in 1756, records details of the blue feline, and in the 1930s a French veterinarian suggested that the breed should have its own scientific name, *Felis catus cartusianorum*. Today's Chartreux should not be confused with the blue British Shorthair or blue European Shorthair. It is massively built, with a very distinctive jowled head, more pronounced in the male than in the female, and is a blue-only breed.

CHARTREUX
One of the true blue cats of the world, the Chartreux is a massive breed with a very gentle nature and a quiet voice.

Breakdown of 100 show points

• Coat	30 points
• Head	25 points
• Body	25 points
• Eye color	10 points
• Tail	10 points

Category Shorthair.
Overall build Medium to large.
Body Solid, firm, and muscular with a broad chest.
Colors Any shade of blue from pale blue gray to deep blue gray, with paler shades preferred. Uniform tone essential.

Head Wide with a narrow, flat plane between the ears, and wide jowls.

Ears Medium size, set high on the head, and slightly flaring, giving an alert expression.

Eyes Large and open, not too rounded, and with the outer corner tilted slightly upward. Eye color is vivid deep yellow to vivid deep copper; the most intense color is preferred.

Coat Dense, with a slightly woolly undercoat and glossy appearance. The double coat makes the hair stand out from the body.

Penalties given for
- Snub nose
- Brown or reddish tinge to coat color
- Any shading, tipping, or ghost tabby markings
- Any trace of green or faded tones in eye color
- Undercoat of unsound color

Nose Broad and straight.

Chin Firm and well developed.

Legs Strong, medium length, and in proportion to the body.

Paws Large.

Tail Medium length in proportion to the body; it may taper and has a rounded tip.

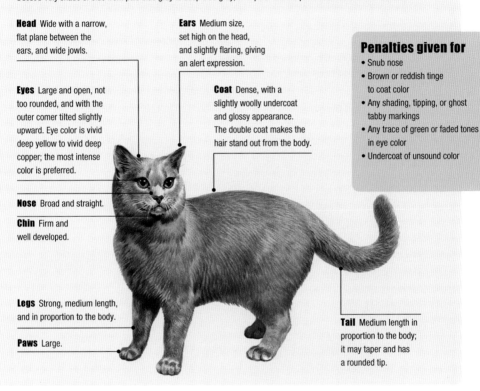

Character and care
Self-assured and affectionate, the Chartreux has always been considered a cat for the connoisseur. It is quiet voiced and will happily live confined to the house. The dense coat needs regular combing to keep the woolly undercoat in good condition, and brushing enhances the way in which the coat stands away from the body—a breed characteristic.

Manx

Legends and fairy tales explaining the origins of this unique tailless breed abound, but modern science agrees that its appearance is due to a mutant dominant gene. The original mutation must have occurred many years ago, for Manx cats have been known since 1900, with a specialist breed club being first established in the UK in 1901.

Although it is an old breed, Manx cats remain rare. The females produce small litters as a direct result of the gene for taillessness. This factor is a semi-lethal gene, and the homozygous Manx—one that inherits the tailless gene from both parents—dies within the womb at an early stage of fetal development.

The Manx that is born alive is the heterozygote—one that inherits only one gene for taillessness, the other member of the gene pair being for a normal tail. Breeders usually cross tailless Manx with normal-tailed Manx offspring to retain the correct body type.

Breakdown of 100 show points

- Body, legs, & paws   30 points
- Taillessness   25 points
- Head & ears   20 points
- Coat   20 points
- Ears   5 points

TORBIE & WHITE MANX
This Manx kitten has adopted the typical natural stance of the breed. Manx kittens are playful and inquisitive, making wonderful pets.

Key characteristics

Category Shorthair.

Overall build Medium.

Body Solidly muscled and compact with sturdy bone structure. The chest is broad and the back short, forming a smooth, continuous arch from the shoulders to the rump, where it curves to give the desirable round look.

Colors Black, blue, red, cream, tortoiseshell, blue-cream, calico, dilute calico, chinchilla silver, shaded silver, black smoke, blue smoke; tabby in brown, blue, red, cream, cameo, silver; torbie in brown, blue, silver; any other color or pattern with the exception of the Himalayan/Siamese pattern. The eye color should be appropriate to the coat color.

Ears Medium size, set wide apart, and turned slightly outward.

Head Round, slightly longer than it is broad, with a rounded forehead, prominent cheeks, and a jowly appearance.

Tail Taillessness is absolute in the perfect Manx, with a definite hollow at the end of the spine where, in a tailed cat, the tail would begin. A rise of bones at the end of the spine is not always penalized, depending on the amount of bone present.

Coat Short, dense, and double, giving a padded quality due to the comparatively long, open outer coat and the close, cottony undercoat.

Eyes Large, round, and full.

Nose Gentle nose dip in profile.

Chin Firm and strong.

Legs Heavily boned. The hind legs are much longer than the forelegs, causing the rump to be higher than the shoulders in the standing cat.

Paws Neat and round.

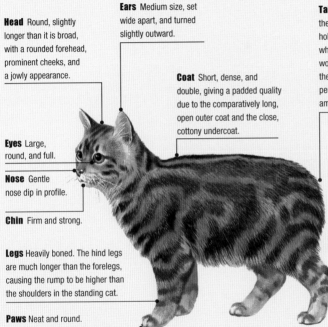

Penalties given for
• Not standing or walking properly

Disqualification features
• Poor physical condition
• Incorrect number of toes
• Color or pattern indicating hybridization

Character and care

Manx cats are highly intelligent, playful, and affectionate, and make ideal and unusual pets. A good specimen generally takes top awards in show when competing against other breeds, particularly if it is easy to handle and performs wells for the judges.

The Manx's double coat repays good feeding and regular grooming. It should be combed through to the roots over the entire body and given a final sheen by polishing with the hands, a grooming mitt, or a silk scarf.

Manx: COLOR VARIETIES

The Manx is accepted in the same colors and patterns as the American Shorthair, with the exception of eye color. In American Shorthair varieties with brilliant gold eye color, the Manx should have eyes of brilliant copper.

RED SPOTTED TABBY
All colors are accepted in the Manx except those in the Himalayan or Siamese pattern.

DILUTE CALICO
The solid body and short back make the typical Manx a sturdy, compact cat. The hind legs are longer than the forelegs, and the rump is firm and rounded.

BROWN TABBY & WHITE
All tabby patterns
are allowed, including
those with the addition
of white areas.
Taillessness is a high-
scoring feature.

Cymric

- The Cymric (pronounced "koom-rik") first appeared in Canada in the 1960s and is a longhaired mutation of the Manx.
- The coat is of medium length, soft and full, giving a padded, heavy look to the body. The same coat colors and patterns are accepted as for the Manx.

Scottish Fold

A litter of otherwise normal kittens born on a farm in Scotland contained the first Scottish Fold in 1961. A shepherd, William Ross, noticed the kitten with the quaint, folded ears and expressed an interest in acquiring such a cat. Two years later, the mother cat, Susie, gave birth to two kittens with folded ears, and William Ross was given one. A breeding program was begun in Britain, but when it was discovered that a small proportion of cats with folded ears also had thickened tails and limbs, the governing registration body banned Scottish Folds from all shows.

The British breeders, who were dedicated to breeding only sound cats, resorted to registering their cats in overseas associations, and the main center of activity for the breed switched to the United States. Today's Scottish Fold cats are bred to British Shorthairs in the UK and to American Shorthairs in the United States, or back to the prick-eared offspring of Folds. The folded ears are due to the action of a single dominant gene, and all Scottish Folds must have at least one fold-eared parent.

BLACK & WHITE SCOTTISH FOLD

This cat illustrates the cap-like attitude of the folded ears in a good example of this breed.

Breakdown of 100 show points

- Ears   30 points
- Tail   20 points
- Eyes   15 points
- Head   15 points
- Body   10 points
- Color   10 points

Key characteristics

Category Shorthair.

Overall build Medium.

Body Firm and well rounded with medium bone.

Colors White, black, blue, red, cream, tortoiseshell, calico, dilute calico, blue-cream, chinchilla silver, shaded silver, shell cameo, shaded cameo, black smoke, blue smoke, cameo smoke, bicolor; classic or mackerel tabby in brown, blue, red, cream, cameo, silver; torbie in brown, blue, silver; any other color or pattern with the exception of those showing evidence of hybridization resulting in the colors chocolate or lavender, the Himalayan pattern, or these combinations with white. The eye color should be appropriate to the coat color. Each variety has identical color requirements to its equivalent variety in the American Shorthair.

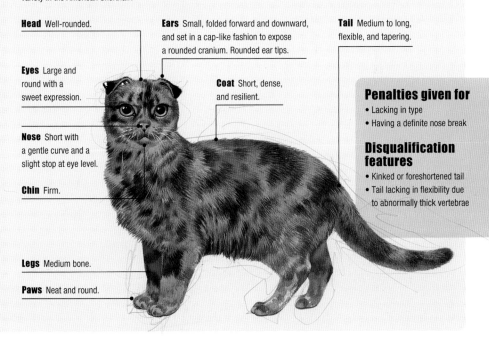

Head Well-rounded.

Ears Small, folded forward and downward, and set in a cap-like fashion to expose a rounded cranium. Rounded ear tips.

Tail Medium to long, flexible, and tapering.

Eyes Large and round with a sweet expression.

Coat Short, dense, and resilient.

Nose Short with a gentle curve and a slight stop at eye level.

Chin Firm.

Legs Medium bone.

Paws Neat and round.

Penalties given for
- Lacking in type
- Having a definite nose break

Disqualification features
- Kinked or foreshortened tail
- Tail lacking in flexibility due to abnormally thick vertebrae

Character and care

The Scottish Fold is a loving, placid, and companionable cat that loves both humans and other pets. The female makes a superb mother, and the kittens are quite precocious.

The short, dense coat is kept in good condition with the minimum of brushing and combing, and the folded ears are kept immaculate by gently cleaning inside the folds with a moistened cotton swab.

European Shorthair

This show breed has been naturally developed from the indigenous cat of continental Europe. Its standard of points is similar to that of the British Shorthair, and it is presumed to be totally free of any admixture of other breeds. The first European Shorthairs were descended from cats introduced to northern Europe by invading armies of Roman soldiers, who brought their cats with them to keep down vermin in their food storage areas.

Breakdown of 100 show points

- Coat   35 points
- Head   25 points
- Body   25 points
- Eye color   10 points
- Condition   5 points

BLACK SILVER TABBY EUROPEAN SHORTHAIR
The spots of this spotted tabby are well marked on the flanks, but tending to form mackerel stripes over the ribs.

Category Shorthair.
Overall build Medium to large but not overlarge.
Body Robust, strong, and muscular with well-developed chest.
Colors White with blue, green, yellow, orange, or odd eyes; black, blue, red, cream, black tortie, blue tortie; smoke: black, blue, red, cream, black tortie, blue tortie; classic, mackerel, or spotted silver or non-silver tabby in black, blue, red, cream, black torbie, blue torbie; bicolor: black, blue, red, cream, black tortie, blue tortie; all bicolors are accepted in the following patterns: tabby, tortie, torbie, van (white coat with colored patches restricted to the extremities) and harlequin (white coat with colored patches over a quarter to half the body surface).

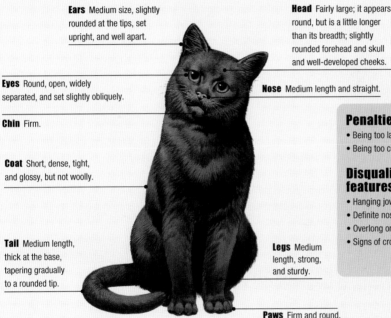

Ears Medium size, slightly rounded at the tips, set upright, and well apart.

Head Fairly large; it appears round, but is a little longer than its breadth; slightly rounded forehead and skull and well-developed cheeks.

Eyes Round, open, widely separated, and set slightly obliquely.

Nose Medium length and straight.

Chin Firm.

Coat Short, dense, tight, and glossy, but not woolly.

Tail Medium length, thick at the base, tapering gradually to a rounded tip.

Legs Medium length, strong, and sturdy.

Paws Firm and round.

Penalties given for
- Being too large in overall size
- Being too cobby or too slender

Disqualification features
- Hanging jowl pouches
- Definite nose stop
- Overlong or woolly coat
- Signs of crossbreeding

Character and care

The European Shorthair is a placid, good-natured breed that makes an ideal family cat. It also accepts the time it spends in the show ring and the demands of being judged with a quiet, dignified tolerance.

The short, dense coat is easy to maintain with a few minutes' daily combing to keep the undercoat in good condition. The eyes and ears should be cleaned regularly with a slightly moistened cotton swab.

European Shorthair:
TABBY & OTHER VARIETIES

*Many European Shorthairs have British Shorthair ancestors
and are found in a similar range of coat colors and patterns.
Tabbies are popular, plus the typy reds and creams,
and pretty blue torties.*

Non-silver tabby

- The six accepted varieties are black tabby, blue tabby, red tabby, cream tabby, black torbie, and blue torbie.
- Classic, mackerel, and spotted coat patterns are accepted. Eye color is green, yellow, or orange.

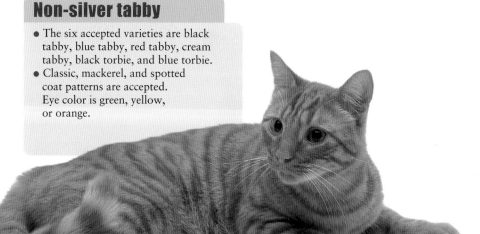

Solid

- In addition to white, solid-colored European Shorthairs may be black, blue, red, or cream. All must have a coat color that is sound to the roots.
- Eye color is green, yellow, or orange.

White

- The coat is pure white without any sign of yellow tingeing or colored hairs.
- There are three subvarieties: eyes of deep blue; green, yellow, or orange eye color; one eye of deep blue and the other eye green, yellow, or orange.

Tortie

- These patched varieties may be either black and red, giving the black tortie, or blue and cream, giving the blue tortie.
- Eye color is green, yellow, or orange.

Silver tabby

- The six accepted varieties are black silver tabby, blue silver tabby, red silver tabby, cream silver tabby, black torbie silver tabby, and blue torbie silver tabby.
- Classic, mackerel, and spotted coat patterns are accepted, with the markings in the main varietal color etched on a base of pure pale silver. Eye color is green, yellow, or orange, but green is preferred.

Smoke

- Cats in this group have a white or silver undercoat, and the six accepted varieties are black smoke, blue smoke, red smoke, cream smoke, black tortie smoke, and blue tortie smoke.
- Eye color is green, yellow, or orange.

Bicolor

- Three patterns are accepted: van, harlequin, and bicolor. The markings may be black, blue, red, cream, black tortie, or blue tortie.

- Nose leather is pink or as expected for the color of the patterned areas. In tabby bicolors, the nose leather is pink or pinkish red outlined with the appropriate color for the patterned areas; in tortie bicolors, the nose leather is patched with pink.
- In van and harlequin patterns, eye color is deep blue, green, yellow, or orange; or odd-eyed with one eye deep blue and the other green, yellow, or orange. In the bicolor pattern, eye color is green, yellow, or orange.

American Shorthair

At the beginning of the twentieth century, an English cat fancier gave a pedigree red tabby British Shorthair male to a friend in the United States, to be mated with some of the indigenous shorthaired felines. This cat was registered in the name of Belle and was the first pedigree cat to appear in the records of the Cat Fanciers' Association. Other British cats followed, including a male silver tabby named Pretty Correct, and the register grew with listings of "home-grown" cats as well as imports. At first, the breed was called the Shorthair, then its name was changed to Domestic Shorthair, and in 1966 it was renamed the American Shorthair. To gain it credence as a natural American breed, registration bodies accepted applications of non-pedigree cats and kittens conforming to the required breed standards, and in 1971 one such cat won the ultimate accolade of the best American Shorthair of the Year in CFA.

Despite the influence of the introduction of the British Shorthair imports in the breeding programs, the American Shorthair has retained its distinctive characteristics.

Because the American Shorthair was developed from domestic cats in all colors and coat patterns, which were crossed with show-quality imported British Shorthairs, today's cats are seen in a wide range of accepted coats. The best known and most popular is undoubtedly the silver tabby, with the classic, marbled,

Breakdown of 100 show points

- Head   30 points
- Tail   25 points
- Color   20 points
- Coat   15 points
- Eye color   10 points

BLUE TABBY AMERICAN SHORTHAIR
This classic tabby, with its typical full-cheeked face, shows a good example of the "M" on the forehead, formed by the clearly marked frown lines.

Key characteristics

Category Shorthair.

Overall build Medium to large.

Body Well-knit, powerful body with well-developed chest and heavy shoulders, but not excessively cobby or rangy.

Colors White, black, blue, red, cream, chinchilla silver, shaded silver, shell cameo, shaded cameo, tortoiseshell, calico, dilute calico, blue-cream, silver tabby, red tabby, brown tabby, blue tabby, cream tabby, cameo tabby, brown torbie, blue torbie, silver torbie, black smoke, blue smoke, cameo smoke, tortoiseshell smoke, bicolor, van bicolor, van calico, van dilute calico.

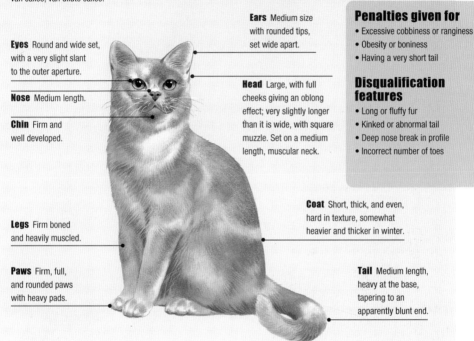

Ears Medium size with rounded tips, set wide apart.

Eyes Round and wide set, with a very slight slant to the outer aperture.

Nose Medium length.

Chin Firm and well developed.

Head Large, with full cheeks giving an oblong effect; very slightly longer than it is wide, with square muzzle. Set on a medium length, muscular neck.

Legs Firm boned and heavily muscled.

Paws Firm, full, and rounded paws with heavy pads.

Coat Short, thick, and even, hard in texture, somewhat heavier and thicker in winter.

Tail Medium length, heavy at the base, tapering to an apparently blunt end.

Penalties given for
- Excessive cobbiness or ranginess
- Obesity or boniness
- Having a very short tail

Disqualification features
- Long or fluffy fur
- Kinked or abnormal tail
- Deep nose break in profile
- Incorrect number of toes

or spotted pattern being the favorites among fanciers. Other tabby colors are also very popular, but each of the accepted varieties has its own following of ardent fans.

Character and care

A cat of very even temperament, the American Shorthair makes an ideal family pet. It is an intelligent and good-natured animal that gets along well with other breeds and with dogs.

Its short, thick coat is quite easy to keep in good condition with a simple grooming routine. Combing keeps the coat neat, and stroking with the hand or a silk scarf imparts a healthy sheen. The eyes and ears are easily cleaned with a cotton swab, and a scratching post helps the indoor cat to trim its claws.

American Shorthair: TABBY VARIETIES

American Shorthair tabby varieties may have the classic or mackerel pattern. In both cases, the markings should be dense and clearly defined.

Red tabby

- The coat, including lips and chin, is red with deep, rich red markings.
- Nose leather and paw pads are brick red; eye color is brilliant gold.

Blue tabby

- The coat, including lips and chin, is pale bluish ivory with very deep blue markings. The whole coat color has warm fawn overtones.
- Nose leather is old rose; paw pads are rose; eye color is brilliant gold.

Brown tabby

- The coat is brilliant coppery brown with dense black markings. The lips and chin should be the same as the rings around the eyes, and the backs of the legs should be black from paw to heel.
- Nose leather is brick red; paw pads are black or brown; eye color is brilliant gold.

Cream tabby

- The coat, including lips and chin, is very pale cream with buff or cream markings sufficiently darker than the base color to afford good contrast.
- Nose leather and paw pads are pink; eye color is brilliant gold.

Cameo tabby

- The coat is soft, delicate off-white with red markings.
- Nose leather and paw pads are rose; eye color is brilliant gold.

Silver tabby

- The coat, including lips and chin, is pale clear silver with dense black markings.
- Nose leather is brick red; paw pads are black; eye color is green or hazel.

Brown torbie

- The coat is brilliant coppery brown with tabby markings of dense black and patches of red and/or light red clearly defined on both body and extremities.
- A blaze of red or light red on the face is desirable. Lips and chin are the same shade as the rings around the eyes; eye color is brilliant gold.

Blue torbie

- The coat, including lips and chin, is pale bluish ivory with tabby markings of very deep blue and patches of cream clearly defined on both body and extremities.
- A blaze of cream on the face is desirable, and warm fawn overtones suffusing the whole body. Eye color is brilliant gold or hazel.

Silver torbie

- The coat, including lips and chin, is pale clear silver with tabby markings of dense black and patches of red and/or light red clearly defined on both body and extremities.
- A blaze of red and/or light red on the face is desirable. Eye color is hazel or brilliant gold.

Snowshoe

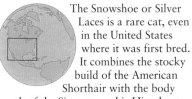

The Snowshoe or Silver Laces is a rare cat, even in the United States where it was first bred. It combines the stocky build of the American Shorthair with the body length of the Siamese, and is Himalayan or Siamese in coloring, but with the white paws that are also found in the Birman.

Two varieties have emerged so far: seal point, with a fawn coat and a paler chest and underside, seal brown points, and snow white paws; and blue point, with a blue white coat and a paler chest and underside, gray blue points, and snow white paws. The eyes are deep blue.

Breakdown of 100 show points

• Pattern	25 points
• Body & tail	25 points
• Head	20 points
• Color	15 points
• Coat	5 points
• Condition	5 points
• Balance	5 points

SNOWSHOE

The Snowshoe is a rare cat and is only recognized in a few associations. It is of the stocky build found in the American Shorthair.

Key characteristics

Category Shorthair.

Overall build Medium.

Body Long and well muscled with a strong back.

Colors Seal point: even pale fawn to cream body; deep seal brown points; deep brown, black, pink, or seal/pink nose leather and paw pads. Blue point: bluish white body; deep steel blue points; slate, pink, or slate/pink nose leather and paw pads. Snow white paws and deep, sparkling blue eyes in both varieties.

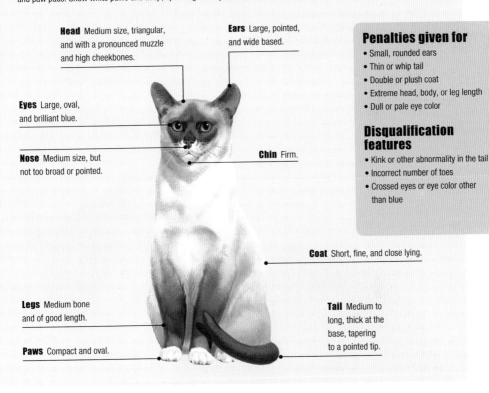

Head Medium size, triangular, and with a pronounced muzzle and high cheekbones.

Ears Large, pointed, and wide based.

Eyes Large, oval, and brilliant blue.

Nose Medium size, but not too broad or pointed.

Chin Firm.

Coat Short, fine, and close lying.

Legs Medium bone and of good length.

Paws Compact and oval.

Tail Medium to long, thick at the base, tapering to a pointed tip.

Penalties given for

- Small, rounded ears
- Thin or whip tail
- Double or plush coat
- Extreme head, body, or leg length
- Dull or pale eye color

Disqualification features

- Kink or other abnormality in the tail
- Incorrect number of toes
- Crossed eyes or eye color other than blue

Character and care

The Snowshoe is a robust and lively cat. It is highly intelligent and loving, and like the Siamese, enjoys human company.

Its coat needs the minimum of grooming, and the white paws may be kept immaculate by dusting with grooming powder from time to time to prevent discoloration.

American Wirehair

In Vermont, in 1966, one of a litter of farm kittens was born with an unusual sparse and wiry coat. An experienced cat breeder acquired the kitten and one of its plain-coated littermates and sent hair samples from both for analysis by a British expert in feline genetics. The coat was of a different type from anything previously encountered in the domestic cat, and a breeding program was soon established to develop the wirehaired trait.

The first wirehaired cat was a red and white male named Adam. He was first mated to his normal-coated littermate, and then to other unrelated shorthaired cats, and from these beginnings a new breed was born. All American Wirehair cats are descended from Adam, and breeding stock has been carefully selected over the years to guarantee refinement and viability of the breed. Championship status was granted by the CFA in 1977.

**BLACK & WHITE
AMERICAN WIREHAIR**
This cat is very well marked, with an inverted "V" on the forehead and the white area continuing right over the chin onto the chest.

Breakdown of 100 show points

- Coat — 45 points
- Head — 25 points
- Type — 20 points
- Color & eye color — 10 points

Key characteristics

Category Wirehair.
Overall build Medium to large. Males are larger than females.
Body Level back and well-rounded rump.
Colors Requirements as for the American Shorthair. White, black, blue, red, cream, tortoiseshell, calico, dilute calico, blue-cream, chinchilla silver, shaded silver, shell cameo, shaded cameo, black smoke, blue smoke, cameo smoke, bicolor; classical or mackerel tabby in brown, blue, red, cream, cameo, silver.

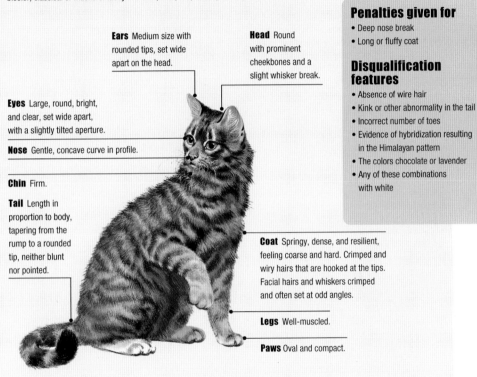

Ears Medium size with rounded tips, set wide apart on the head.

Head Round with prominent cheekbones and a slight whisker break.

Eyes Large, round, bright, and clear, set wide apart, with a slightly tilted aperture.

Nose Gentle, concave curve in profile.

Chin Firm.

Tail Length in proportion to body, tapering from the rump to a rounded tip, neither blunt nor pointed.

Coat Springy, dense, and resilient, feeling coarse and hard. Crimped and wiry hairs that are hooked at the tips. Facial hairs and whiskers crimped and often set at odd angles.

Legs Well-muscled.

Paws Oval and compact.

Penalties given for
- Deep nose break
- Long or fluffy coat

Disqualification features
- Absence of wire hair
- Kink or other abnormality in the tail
- Incorrect number of toes
- Evidence of hybridization resulting in the Himalayan pattern
- The colors chocolate or lavender
- Any of these combinations with white

Character and care
The Wirehair is said by its owners to rule the home and cats of other breeds with an "iron paw," but to make a devoted parent. It is affectionate and playful, with a strongly independent character.

The unusual wiry coat is easy to maintain in peak condition by correct feeding and needs minimal grooming.

Exotic Shorthair

In the development of British and American Shorthairs, and during the introduction of alternative color factors in the Persian, breeders occasionally mated together pedigree cats of longhaired and shorthaired varieties. This was generally done as a single exercise, the offspring being backcrossed to the main breed in successive generations to strengthen the desired traits.

During the 1960s, cats of mixed Shorthair and Persian lineage were, with the approval of the board of the CFA, given the breed name Exotic Shorthair.

The breed is, in essence, a short-coated version of the typical Persian, with the conformation of the latter, but the added bonus of a coat that is relatively easy to care for. The coat stands out from the body and is longer than that of the British or American Shorthair breeds.

SILVER TABBY EXOTIC SHORTHAIR
The intensity of the dark tabby markings is reduced when etched on a silver base coat.

Breakdown of 100 show points

- Head   30 points
- Coat   20 points
- Type   20 points
- Color   20 points
- Eye color   10 points

Key characteristics

Category Shorthair.

Overall build Medium to large.

Body Cobby, with a deep chest, massive shoulders and rump, and a level back.

Colors White with blue, copper, or odd eyes; black, blue, chocolate, lilac, red, cream; classic, mackerel, or spotted tabby in silver, brown, blue, chocolate, lilac, red, cream; torbie: brown, blue, chocolate, lilac; tortoiseshell, blue-cream, calico, dilute calico; bicolor, van bicolor, and van tricolor: any recognized color with white; smoke: any recognized color with silver white undercoat; tipped: any recognized color with white undercoat and color restricted to very tips of hair; colorpoint in solid or tabby form: seal, blue, red, cream, lilac, chocolate.

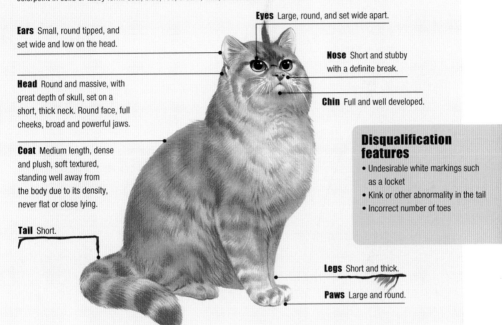

Eyes Large, round, and set wide apart.

Ears Small, round tipped, and set wide and low on the head.

Nose Short and stubby with a definite break.

Head Round and massive, with great depth of skull, set on a short, thick neck. Round face, full cheeks, broad and powerful jaws.

Chin Full and well developed.

Coat Medium length, dense and plush, soft textured, standing well away from the body due to its density, never flat or close lying.

Disqualification features

- Undesirable white markings such as a locket
- Kink or other abnormality in the tail
- Incorrect number of toes

Tail Short.

Legs Short and thick.

Paws Large and round.

Character and care

In temperament, the Exotic Shorthair is quiet, gentle, and placid. It is an ideal show cat, easy to prepare for the show ring, and enjoys being handled and admired.

The medium length coat is quite easy to comb through, and being groomed from the tail toward the head encourages the plush fur to stand away from the body. Body condition and shining fur is achieved by correct feeding, and the eyes and ears are kept immaculate by gentle cleaning with a cotton swab.

Exotic Shorthair: SOLID VARIETIES

Solid-colored Exotic Shorthairs are bred to a very exacting standard and are penalized for having incorrect or extremely pale eye colors, flecks of incorrect color in the irises, or oriental or slanted eyes.

Blue

- The coat is an even shade of blue, sound to the roots, stretching from the nose to the tip of the tail. Lighter shades are preferred.
- Nose leather and paw pads are blue; eye color is brilliant copper.

White

- The coat is pure, glistening white. Nose leather and paw pads are pink.
- Eye color is deep blue or brilliant copper. Odd-eyed whites should have one blue and one copper eye of equal color intensity.

Black

- The dense coal black coat should be sound from roots to tips of fur.
- Nose leather is black; paw pads are black or brown; eye color is brilliant copper.

Cream

- The coat is an even shade of buff cream throughout, with no shading or markings. Lighter shades are preferred.
- Nose leather and paw pads are pink; eye color is brilliant copper.

Red

- The coat is deep, rich, brilliant red without any shading, markings, or ticking. The lips and chin should be the same color as the coat.
- Nose leather and paw pads are brick red; eye color is brilliant copper.

Chocolate

- The coat is warm-toned medium to dark chocolate, free from shading or markings.
- Nose leather and paw pads are chocolate; eye color is copper or orange.

Lilac

- The coat is a warm-toned, even shade of lilac.
- Nose leather and paw pads are lilac; eye color is copper or orange.

Exotic Shorthair: BICOLOR VARIETIES

Bicolored Exotic Shorthairs should have clear and well-distributed patches of color.

Bicolor

- The coat is white with unbrindled patches of either black, blue, red, or cream, as seen in the American Shorthair.
- Nose leather and paw pads correspond with the varietal color; eye color is brilliant copper.

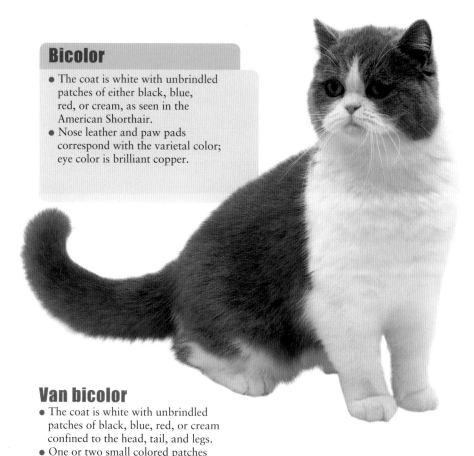

Van bicolor

- The coat is white with unbrindled patches of black, blue, red, or cream confined to the head, tail, and legs.
- One or two small colored patches on the body are allowed.

Van tricolor

- The coat is white with unbrindled patches of black and red confined to the head, tail, and legs.
- Up to three small colored patches on the body are allowed.

Van dilute calico

- The coat is white with unbrindled patches of blue and cream confined to the head, tail, and legs.
- One or two small colored patches on the body are allowed.

Exotic Shorthair:
TABBY & OTHER VARIETIES

The Exotic Shorthair is the ideal breed for the owner who craves for a cat with true Persian type, but does not have the time necessary to care for the Persian coat.

Tabby

- Classic, mackerel, and spotted patterns are accepted in silver, brown, blue, chocolate, lilac, red, and cream.
- Color requirements are identical to the equivalent varieties in the American or British Shorthair, except for eye color, which is brilliant copper.

Torbie

- Torbie Exotics are accepted in brown, blue, chocolate, and lilac.
- Color requirements and eye color is as for the tabby.

Tortoiseshell

- The coat is black with clearly defined, well-broken, unbrindled patches of red and light red on the body and extremities.
- A red or light red blaze on the face is desirable. Eye color is brilliant copper.

Blue-cream

- The coat is blue with clearly defined, well-broken patches of solid cream on the body and the extremities.
- Eye color is brilliant copper.

Calico

- The coat is white with unbrindled patches of black and red, with white predominant on the underparts.
- Eye color is brilliant copper.

Dilute calico

- The coat is white with unbrindled patches of light to medium blue and pale cream, with white predominant on the underparts.
- Eye color is brilliant copper.

Exotic Shorthair:
TABBY & OTHER VARIETIES *continued*

Shaded silver

- The coat is pure white heavily shaded with black, graduating from dark on the spine to white on the chin, chest, stomach, and under the tail. The legs are the same tone as the face.
- Rims of the eyes, lips, and nose are outlined with black. Nose leather is brick red; paw pads are black; eye color is green or blue green.

Chinchilla silver

- The coat is pure white tipped with black on the back, flanks, head, and tail. The legs may be slightly tipped. The chin, ear tufts, stomach, and chest are pure white.
- Rims of the eyes, lips, and nose are outlined with black. Nose leather is brick red; paw pads are black; eye color is green or blue green.

Chinchilla golden

- The coat is rich, warm cream tipped with seal brown on the back, flanks, head, and tail. The legs may be slightly tipped. The chin, ear tufts, stomach, and chest are cream.
- Rims of the eyes, lips, and nose are outlined with seal brown. Nose leather is deep rose; paw pads are seal brown; eye color is green or blue green.

Shaded golden

- The coat is rich, warm cream heavily shaded with seal brown, graduating from dark on the spine to cream on the chin, chest, stomach, and under the tail. The legs are the same tone as the face.
- Rims of the eyes, lips, and nose are outlined with seal brown. Nose leather is deep rose; paw pads are seal brown; eye color is green or blue green.

Smoke

- The smoke Exotic may be of any color accepted in the Exotic group, but instead of being sound in color from tips to roots, the base of each hair is silvery white. There must be no tabby markings.
- Nose leather and paw pads should correspond with the coat color; eye color is copper, orange, or deep gold.

Colorpoint

- The body is pale with the varietal color on the face, tail, legs, and paws. The six accepted colors are seal, blue, red, cream, lilac, and chocolate in solid and tabby forms.
- Nose leather and paw pads correspond with the points color; eye color is decidedly blue.

Shaded tortoiseshell

- The coat is white heavily shaded with black tipping and clearly defined patches of red- and light red-tipped hairs in the tortie pattern.
- A blaze of red or light red tipping on the face is desirable. Nose leather and paw pads are black, pink, or mottled; eye color is brilliant copper.

Tipped

- The tipping may be of any color accepted in the Persian varieties. The undercoat must be as white as possible and the tips of each hair lightly colored.
- In cats with black tipping, nose leather is brick red and paw pads are black or seal brown. In other colors, both correspond with the coat color.

Foreign
Shorthaired Breeds

Abyssinian

No evidence exists to connect an Abyssinian cat, recorded as having been taken from Ethiopia to England in 1868, with today's pedigree cats. Recognized as a true breed in 1882, the Abyssinian was also known as the Spanish, Russian, Ticked, Hare, or Bunny Cat—it was once thought that it had resulted from a cross between a cat and wild rabbit.

The modern Abyssinian is a well-established breed worldwide.

It has been referred to as the Child of the Gods because of its close resemblance to the sacred cats of the ancient Egyptians. Whatever their color, all Abyssinian cats have unusual ticked coats, known as the agouti, or wild-type, pattern. Selective breeding over many generations has resulted in a reduction of the natural tabby bars normally found on the face, neck, tail, and underparts, so that today's show cat has a clear, glowing, ticked coat, rather like that of a Belgian hare.

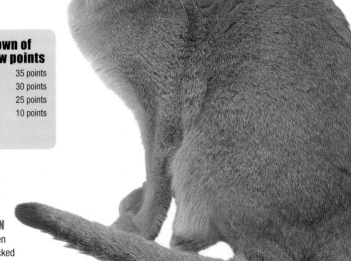

Breakdown of 100 show points

• Color	35 points
• Body	30 points
• Head	25 points
• Coat	10 points

RUDDY ABYSSINIAN
The rich golden brown coat ticked with bands of black gives the ruddy its unusual appearance.

Key characteristics

Category Foreign shorthair.
Overall build Medium.
Body Long, lithe, and muscular but graceful.
Colors Ruddy (usual), blue, red (sorrel), chocolate, lilac, fawn, black silver, blue silver. Note that not all color varieties are recognized by all associations.

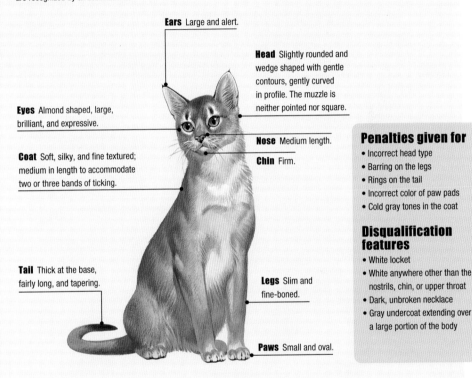

Ears Large and alert.

Head Slightly rounded and wedge shaped with gentle contours, gently curved in profile. The muzzle is neither pointed nor square.

Eyes Almond shaped, large, brilliant, and expressive.

Nose Medium length.

Chin Firm.

Coat Soft, silky, and fine textured; medium in length to accommodate two or three bands of ticking.

Tail Thick at the base, fairly long, and tapering.

Legs Slim and fine-boned.

Paws Small and oval.

Penalties given for

- Incorrect head type
- Barring on the legs
- Rings on the tail
- Incorrect color of paw pads
- Cold gray tones in the coat

Disqualification features

- White locket
- White anywhere other than the nostrils, chin, or upper throat
- Dark, unbroken necklace
- Gray undercoat extending over a large portion of the body

The Abyssinian is another foreign shorthaired breed that is judged by slightly different standards in Europe and North America. The American Abyssinian has a shorter head and a more rounded profile than its European counterpart.

Character and care

The Abyssinian cat is typically quiet and gentle. It can be shy and reserved, mistrusting strangers, but it generally gets along well with other cats and adores its owner.

The coat is simple to keep immaculate with the minimum of grooming. The large ears must be kept clean at all times by regular use of moistened cotton swabs.

Abyssinian: RUDDY & OTHER VARIETIES

Ruddy is the normal coat color of the Abyssinian. It is genetically black, the rich golden hairs having two or three bands of black ticking. The color ruddy is also referred to as "usual" in the UK, and the color red as sorrel.

Red

- The coat is bright, warm, coppery red with chocolate brown ticking; the base color is deep apricot. The tail tip, ear tips, eye rims, backs of feet, and toe tufts are red brown.
- Nose leather is pale red and may be outlined with red brown; paw pads are cinnamon to chocolate; eye color is as for the ruddy.

Ruddy

- The coat is warm ruddy brown with black ticking; the base color is deep apricot or orange. The tail tip, ear tips, and eye rims are black.
- Nose leather is brick red and may be outlined with black; paw pads, backs of feet, and toe tufts are seal brown or black; eye color is gold or green, with rich, deep colors preferred.

Black silver

- The coat is pure silver white with black ticking; the base color is pure silver white. The tail tip and eye rims are black; the ear tips, paw pads, backs of feet, and toe tufts are black or seal brown.
- Nose leather is brick red and may be outlined with black; eye color is as for the ruddy.

Fawn

- The coat is dull beige with deep, warm fawn ticking; the base color is pale cream. The tail tip, ear tips, backs of feet, and toe tufts are dark warm cream; the eye rims are old rose.
- Nose leather is pink and may be outlined with old rose; paw pads are pink; eye color is as for the ruddy.

Blue

- The coat is warm blue gray with dark, steel blue gray ticking; the base color is pale fawn/cream. The tail tip, ear tips, backs of feet, and toe tufts are dark steel blue gray; the eye rims are blue gray.
- Nose leather is old rose and may be outlined with blue gray; paw pads are old rose/blue gray; eye color is as for the ruddy.

Blue silver

- The coat is pure silver white with dark steel blue gray ticking; the base color is pure silver white. The tail tip, ear tips, eye rims, backs of feet, and toe tufts are dark steel blue gray.
- Nose leather is old rose and may be outlined with dark steel blue gray; paw pads are old rose or blue gray; eye color is as for the ruddy.

Somali

This breed is the longhaired version of the Abyssinian cat, and its coat color is typically Abyssinian. It was thought that the long coat was due to a spontaneous mutation occurring within the Abyssinian breed, but genetic investigation of the history of the Somali showed that the gene for long hair was probably introduced when cats of Abyssinian type and lineage were outcrossed to others in the early days of breeding and showing.

When the first long-coated kittens appeared in otherwise normal litters of Abyssinian kittens, they were discarded and given away as pets, but later, having seen some of these cats at maturity when the full beauty of the ticked longhaired coat was apparent, breeders decided to develop the longhaired Abyssinian as a separate variety. A worldwide network of breeders—in North America, Europe, New Zealand, and Australia—worked

Breakdown of 100 show points

- Coat — 35 points
- Body — 25 points
- Head — 10 points
- Ears — 10 points
- Eyes — 10 points
- Condition — 10 points

BLUE SILVER SOMALI

The white base coat is ticked with blue to give a sparkling silvery blue gray coat pattern. As in all Somali varieties, the ears and tail color should match the ticking.

Key characteristics

Category Foreign longhair.

Overall build Medium to large.

Body Medium length, firm bone structure, lithe, and muscular.

Colors As for the Abyssinian: ruddy (usual), blue, red (sorrel), chocolate, lilac, fawn; silver varieties in all these colors. Note that not all color varieties are recognized by all associations.

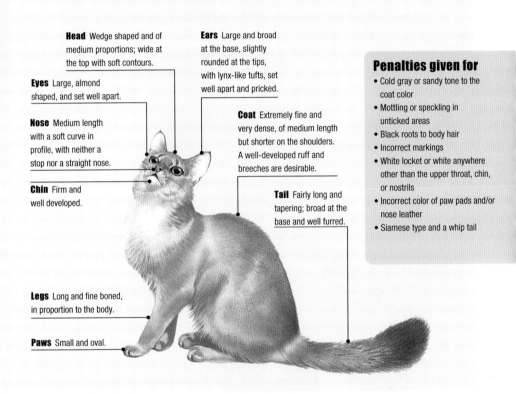

Head Wedge shaped and of medium proportions; wide at the top with soft contours.

Eyes Large, almond shaped, and set well apart.

Nose Medium length with a soft curve in profile, with neither a stop nor a straight nose.

Chin Firm and well developed.

Ears Large and broad at the base, slightly rounded at the tips, with lynx-like tufts, set well apart and pricked.

Coat Extremely fine and very dense, of medium length but shorter on the shoulders. A well-developed ruff and breeches are desirable.

Tail Fairly long and tapering; broad at the base and well furred.

Legs Long and fine boned, in proportion to the body.

Paws Small and oval.

Penalties given for

- Cold gray or sandy tone to the coat color
- Mottling or speckling in unticked areas
- Black roots to body hair
- Incorrect markings
- White locket or white anywhere other than the upper throat, chin, or nostrils
- Incorrect color of paw pads and/or nose leather
- Siamese type and a whip tail

together and agreed on Somali as the cat's name. The breed was granted full championship status by the CFA in 1978.

Character and care

Like the Abyssinian, the Somali is gentle and receptive to quiet handling and affection. It is soft voiced, playful, and athletic, and makes a perfect companion pet.

The coat, though full, is not woolly and is therefore very easy to groom. The full ruff and tail need regular combing through, and the large ears must be gently cleaned and kept free from dust.

Somali: NON-SILVER VARIETIES

Although different cat associations have their own rules for acceptance of new varieties, the Somali is recognized in most of the regular Abyssinian color varieties by most registering bodies. Like the Abyssinian, the ruddy variety may be referred to as the usual, and the red as sorrel.

Ruddy

- The coat is rich, glowing golden brown ticked with black. The tail is tipped with black, and the ears with black or dark brown.
- Nose leather is tile red; paw pads, heels, and toe tufts are black or dark brown.

Lilac

- The pinkish dove gray coat is ticked with a deeper shade of the same color; the base coat is paler. This variety has a powdered effect to the coat. The ears and tail are tipped with the same color as the ticking.
- Nose leather is pinkish mauve; pinkish mauve paw pads have deeper dove gray between the toes and extending up the heels; toe tufts are deep dove gray.

Blue

- Any shade of blue ticked with darker blue is allowed; the base coat is cream or oatmeal. The ears and tail are tipped with the same color as the ticking.
- Nose leather is blue mauve; blue mauve paw pads have deeper blue between the toes and extending up the heels; toe tufts are deep blue.

Chocolate

- The coat is rich, golden, coppery brown ticked with dark chocolate; the base coat is paler. The ears and tail are tipped with the same color as the ticking.
- Nose leather is pinkish chocolate; paw pads are chocolate with darker chocolate between the toes and extending up the heels; toe tufts are dark chocolate.

Fawn

- The warm fawn coat is ticked with a deeper shade of the same color; the base coat is paler. The ears and tail are tipped with the same color as the ticking.
- Nose leather is pink; pinkish mauve paw pads have deep fawn between the toes and extending up the heels; toe tufts are deep fawn.

Red

- The warm, glowing copper coat is ticked with chocolate; the base coat is deep apricot. The ears and tail are tipped with chocolate.
- Nose leather is pink; paw pads are pink with chocolate between the toes and extending up the heels; toe tufts are chocolate.

Somali: SILVER VARIETIES

A yellowish effect on the body, known as "fawning," is an undesirable trait in the silver series of Somali cats. It occurs particularly in the ruddy silver, and in blue silver varieties especially on the face and paws.

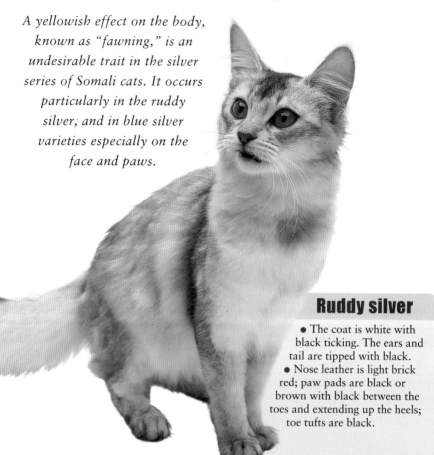

Ruddy silver

- The coat is white with black ticking. The ears and tail are tipped with black.
- Nose leather is light brick red; paw pads are black or brown with black between the toes and extending up the heels; toe tufts are black.

Blue silver

- The coat is white with blue ticking, giving an overall sparkling silvery gray effect. The ears and tail are tipped with blue.
- Nose leather is blue mauve; blue mauve paw pads have blue between the toes, extending up the heels; toe tufts are blue.

Chocolate silver

- The coat is white with dark chocolate ticking, giving an overall sparkling silvery chocolate effect. The ears and tail are tipped with dark chocolate.
- Nose leather is pinkish chocolate; paw pads are chocolate with dark chocolate between the toes and extending up the heels; ear tufts are dark chocolate.

Red silver

- The coat is white with chocolate ticking, giving the overall sparkling silvery peach effect. The ears and tail are tipped with chocolate.
- Nose leather is pink; pink paw pads have chocolate brown between the toes and extending up the heels; toe tufts are dark chocolate.

Lilac silver

- The coat is white with dove gray ticking, giving an overall sparkling dove gray effect.
- Nose leather is pinkish mauve; pinkish mauve paw pads have dove gray between the toes and extending up the heels; toe tufts are dove gray.

Fawn silver

- The coat is white with fawn ticking, giving an overall sparkling silvery fawn effect. The ears and tail are tipped with fawn.
- Nose leather is pink; pinkish mauve paw pads have fawn between the toes and extending up the heels; toe tufts are fawn.

Russian Blue

The very handsome and unique Russian Blue is a natural breed with a unique combination of conformation, color, and coat that make it a striking animal.

The first Russian Blue cats are thought to have originated near the White Sea port of Archangel, just outside the Arctic Circle, and were carried as trade goods by merchant sailors on ships trading with England. The cats were shown extensively in England during the latter part of the nineteenth century, but differed from those of today in having bright orange eyes. The breed was exhibited under a number of names, including the Spanish Blue, the Archangel, and the Maltese. In the first cat shows, all shorthaired blue cats competed in one class, regardless of type. In 1912, the Russian Blue was given its own classes, but during World War II the breed almost became extinct, being saved only by outcrossing to Siamese. Cats of foreign type were then shown as Russian Blues, but eventually breeders made a coordinated attempt to return to the pre-war characteristics of the breed, and in 1966 the show standard was changed to state specifically that Siamese type was undesirable in the Russian Blue.

Breakdown of 100 show points

- Coat   30 points
- Head & ears   20 points
- Body, legs, & tail   20 points
- Eyes   15 points
- Color   15 points

RUSSIAN BLUE

A natural breed with a long and interesting history, the Russian Blue has an elegant and graceful appearance.

Key characteristics

Category Foreign shorthair.

Overall build Medium.

Body Fine boned, long, lithe, and muscular.

Colors Blue only (some associations in Australia and New Zealand recognize a black Russian and a white Russian). The coat is clear, even blue, with silver-tipped guard hairs giving the cat an overall lustrous silvery sheen. Lighter blue shades are preferred in the US, and medium blue shades in the UK. Nose leather is slate gray; paw pads are lavender pink or mauve; eye color is vivid green.

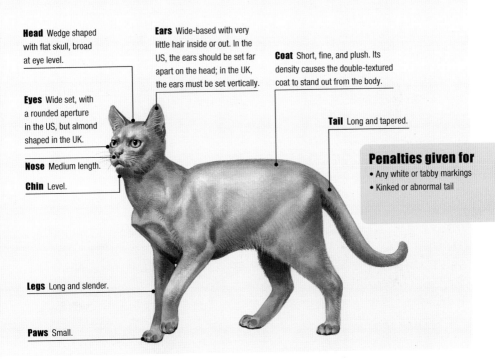

Head Wedge shaped with flat skull, broad at eye level.

Ears Wide-based with very little hair inside or out. In the US, the ears should be set far apart on the head; in the UK, the ears must be set vertically.

Coat Short, fine, and plush. Its density causes the double-textured coat to stand out from the body.

Eyes Wide set, with a rounded aperture in the US, but almond shaped in the UK.

Tail Long and tapered.

Nose Medium length.

Chin Level.

Penalties given for
- Any white or tabby markings
- Kinked or abnormal tail

Legs Long and slender.

Paws Small.

Maltese or Russian Blue cats are recorded in the United States as long ago as 1900, but only in 1947 did breeders really start work with these unique cats, and even today the breed is rare in the show rings of the world.

Character and care

The Russian Blue has a delightful temperament, being quiet voiced and very affectionate. It does not like to be left alone for long periods and needs the company either of a human being or other pets.

The unique coat, with its short, thick double fur, should be regularly combed through and may be stroked both ways without exposing the blue skin. The sparsely furred ears must be kept clean at all times.

Korat

The breed originated in Thailand where it is called Si-Sawat, a descriptive compound word referring to its silver gray coat and luminous, light green eyes. The thirteenth-century *Book of Cat Poems* in the National Library of Bangkok illustrates the breed with the caption: "The cat Mal-ed has a body like Doklao, the hairs are smooth with roots like clouds and tips like silver, the eyes shine like dewdrops on a lotus leaf." *Mal-ed* refers to the seed of the "look sawat," a silvery gray fruit lightly tinged with green. *Dok* is a flower, and *lao* a plant with silver-tipped flowers. Highly prized in its native land, the Si-Sawat is considered a harbinger of good fortune, and a pair of these cats is a traditional wedding gift, intended to bring longevity, wealth, and happiness to the couple.

First exhibited in London in 1896, the Korat was disqualified, being judged as a Siamese cat and not having the desired fawn coat, dark points, and blue eyes. In 1959 Korat cats arrived in the United

Breakdown of 100 show points

• Head	25 points
• Body	25 points
• Color	25 points
• Eyes	15 points
• Coat	10 points

KORAT
A natural breed discovered in Thailand, the Korat was considered a good luck charm, and often given as a wedding gift.

Key characteristics

Category Foreign shorthair.
Overall build Small to medium. Females are daintier than males.
Body Muscular and supple, midway between a Shorthair and Siamese in type.
Colors Blue only. The coat is silvery blue tipped with silver; nose leather and lips are dark blue or lavender; paw pads are dark blue ranging to lavender with a pinkish tinge; eye color is preferably luminous green but amber is acceptable.

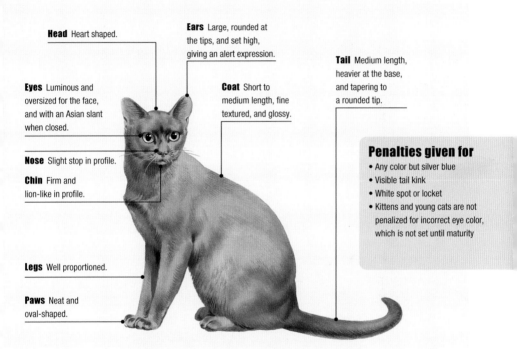

Head Heart shaped.

Ears Large, rounded at the tips, and set high, giving an alert expression.

Tail Medium length, heavier at the base, and tapering to a rounded tip.

Eyes Luminous and oversized for the face, and with an Asian slant when closed.

Coat Short to medium length, fine textured, and glossy.

Nose Slight stop in profile.

Chin Firm and lion-like in profile.

Legs Well proportioned.

Paws Neat and oval-shaped.

Penalties given for

- Any color but silver blue
- Visible tail kink
- White spot or locket
- Kittens and young cats are not penalized for incorrect eye color, which is not set until maturity

States, where they were officially recognized in 1966. The cat fanciers of South Africa and Australia officially accepted the breed in 1968 and 1969 respectively, but the UK's Governing Council of the Cat Fancy delayed recognition until 1975 and then withheld championship status. In 1983, the Cat Association of Britain finally accepted the Korat for full status, and the UK's first champion was chosen by judges from England, Belgium, and Australia.

Character and care

The Korat is a dainty, quiet-voiced little cat, generally alert, inquisitive, and affectionate. Its short, dense coat is easily cared for with a weekly brushing and buffing with a silk scarf.

Havana Brown

This unique, manmade breed came into being when British breeders were working with Russian Blue and shorthair crossmatings during the early 1950s, and solid-colored chocolate brown kittens were occasionally produced. At that time, the science of feline color genetics was in its infancy, but it was soon established that chocolate kittens could only occur when both parents carried the chocolate factor, and when two chocolate cats were mated, chocolate kittens always resulted.

Cats from these early matings were developed in the UK as the Chestnut Brown Foreign Shorthair and were outcrossed to Siamese to establish

Breakdown of 100 show points

- Color   35 points
- Head   25 points
- Body & neck   15 points
- Coat   10 points
- Eyes   5 points
- Tail   5 points
- Legs & feet   5 points

HAVANA BROWN
Large, pricked ears and vivid green oval eyes give the Havana Brown its typical, sweet expression. The smooth, lustrous body is evenly colored in warm brown.

Category Foreign shorthair.

Overall build Medium.

Body Firm, muscular, and of medium length.

Colors Warm brown only. The coat is a rich, even shade of warm brown throughout. Kittens are not penalized for showing ghost tabby markings. Nose leather is brown with a rosy flush; paw pads must have a rosy tone; eye color is vivid green.

Head Slightly longer than it is wide, with a distinct change in slope at eye level when viewed in profile.

Ears Large, round-tipped, and wide set but not flaring and slightly pricked forward, giving an alert appearance.

Eyes Oval shaped.

Nose Rounded muzzle with a definite break on each side behind the whisker pads.

Chin Well developed.

Coat Short to medium length, smooth, and lustrous.

Penalties given for
- Incorrect color of nose leather, paw pads, or eyes
- Kinked tail
- White locket or button

Legs In proportion to body.

Paws Neat and oval.

Tail Medium length, tapering gently to a slightly pointed tip.

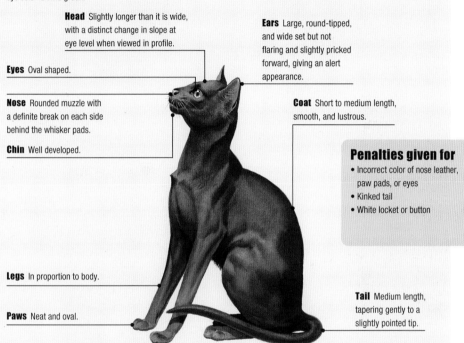

oriental type and conformation. Others were sent to the United States to establish a new breed and were bred to a unique standard of points as the Havana Brown.

Character and care
This breed is highly intelligent, affectionate, and very agile. Less vocal than the Siamese, it is playful and craves human company. It makes a superb pet.

The coat is easy to maintain in good condition with the minimum of grooming. Combing removes any loose hairs, and buffing with the hand or a silk scarf produces a sheen on the glossy brown coat.

Egyptian Mau

Not to be confused with cats of the same name bred experimentally in the UK during the 1960s and now called Oriental tabbies, the Egyptian Mau is a naturally occurring breed in Egypt. The first to leave their native land were taken to Italy from Cairo in 1953 by Princess Natalie Troubetskoye. She then took offspring of the cats with her to the United States in 1956. It is a spotted cat, very similar to those pictured in ancient Egyptian scrolls and cartoons. The name Mau is borrowed from the ancient Egyptian civilization, where it meant cat. It gained official recognition from the CFF in 1968 and finally from the CFA in 1977.

Breakdown of 100 show points

- Body   25 points
- Pattern   25 points
- Color   25 points
- Head   20 points
- Coat   5 points

SILVER EGYPTIAN MAU

The silver Egyptian Mau has clear markings in dark charcoal on a pale silver ground color. The green eyes complete the rather exotic effect.

Key characteristics

Category Foreign shorthair.
Overall build Medium.
Body Medium length and muscular but graceful.
Colors Silver: pale silver ground color; dark charcoal markings contrasting with ground color; backs of the ears are grayish pink tipped with black; nose, lips, and eyes are outlined in black; upper throat, chin, and around the nostrils is pale clear silver, appearing white; nose leather is brick red; paw pads are black; eye color is light green. Bronze: light bronze ground color with creamy ivory underparts; dark brown markings against the ground color; backs of the ears are tawny pink tipped with dark brown; nose, lips, and eyes are outlined in dark brown, with ocher on the bridge of the nose; upper throat, chin, and around the nostrils are pale creamy white; nose leather is brick red; paw pads are black or dark brown; eye color is light green. Smoke: charcoal gray ground color with silver undercoat; jet black markings plainly visible; nose, lips, and eyes are outlined in jet black; upper throat, chin, and around the nostrils are lightest in color; nose leather and pads are black: eye color is light green.

Ears Medium to large, alert, and slightly pointed. Inner ear delicate shell pink. Ears tufts accepted.

Eyes Large and almond shaped.

Nose Short.

Chin Medium size.

Legs In proportion to body, with higher hind legs.

Paws Small and slightly oval.

Head Slightly rounded wedge of medium length. Muzzle neither short nor pointed.

Coat Silky and fine, dense and resilient to the touch, with a lustrous sheen. Medium length hair, with two or more bands of ticking, separated by lighter bands.

Tail Medium length, thick at the base, and slightly tapered.

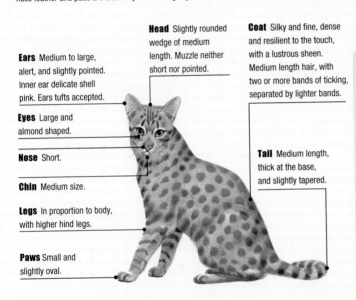

Penalties given for
- Short or round head
- Pointed muzzle
- Small, round, or oriental eyes
- Cobby or oriental body type
- Short or whip tail
- Incorrect Mau pattern
- Poor condition
- Amber cast in eyes of cats over one and a half years of age

Disqualification features
- Lack of spots
- Blue eye color
- Kinked or abnormal tail

Character and care
Rather shy but very loving, the Mau tends to attach its affections to only one or two people. It is naturally active and may be taught one or two tricks. It is delicate of constitution and does not adapt well to cold temperatures or to the change of seasons.

Although the short coat is easy to keep in good condition, regular combing is required to remove dead hair.

Ocicat

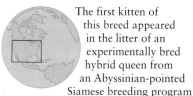

The first kitten of this breed appeared in the litter of an experimentally bred hybrid queen from an Abyssinian-pointed Siamese breeding program mated with a chocolate-pointed Siamese male. The kitten, which was called Tonga, reminded its breeder of a baby ocelot, and she decided to produce similar cats, which were eventually recognized as a separate breed called Ocicats.

Apart from the Ocicat itself, outcrosses to Abyssinian, American Shorthair, and Siamese are allowed in the pedigree. The Ocicat is a rather large but well-proportioned cat, muscular and agile, with a typically "wild cat" appearance. It is remarkable for its very clear spotted pattern and its striking golden eyes.

Breakdown of 100 show points

- Head — 25 points
- Pattern — 25 points
- Body — 20 points
- Coat — 20 points
- Eye color — 5 points
- Condition — 5 points

BLACK SILVER SPOTTED OCICAT
This kitten is very well patterned with clear spots, the correct head markings, and pleasing type.

Key characteristics

Category Foreign shorthair.
Overall build Medium to large.
Body Long, solid, and athletic, with substantial bone and muscle structure.
Colors Black spotted, blue spotted, chocolate spotted, lilac spotted, cinnamon spotted, fawn spotted, black silver spotted, blue silver spotted, chocolate silver spotted, lilac silver spotted, cinnamon silver spotted, fawn silver spotted. All colors should be clear. The lightest color is on the face, around the eyes, on the chin, and the lower jaw; the darkest color is at the tip of the tail. Markings on the face, legs, and tail may be darker than those on the body. The ground color may be darker on the saddle and lighter on the underside, chin, and lower jaw. All hairs except those on the tip of the tail are banded. Within the markings, hairs are tipped with the darker color; hairs in the ground color are tipped with a lighter color.

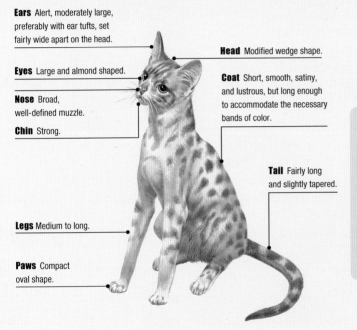

Ears Alert, moderately large, preferably with ear tufts, set fairly wide apart on the head.

Head Modified wedge shape.

Eyes Large and almond shaped.

Nose Broad, well-defined muzzle.

Chin Strong.

Coat Short, smooth, satiny, and lustrous, but long enough to accommodate the necessary bands of color.

Tail Fairly long and slightly tapered.

Legs Medium to long.

Paws Compact oval shape.

Penalties given for
- Faint, blurred, or incorrect markings
- Coarseness of body type

Disqualification features
- White locket
- Any white except as specified in the standard

Character and care
Ocicats are loving and gentle, inquisitive and playful, and make excellent pets.

Their coats should be groomed by gentle brushing and combing through on a regular basis to remove dead hair.

Bengal

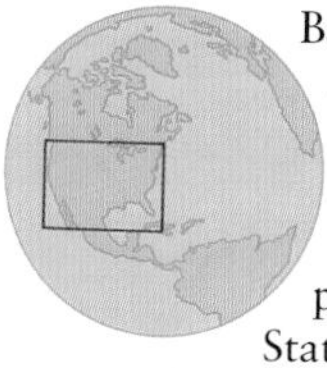

Based on crosses between Asian leopard cats that live wild in southeastern Asia and domestic cats, the Bengal was first produced in the United States. It seems to have preserved the self-assurance and confidence of the Asian leopard cat in conjunction with the affectionate disposition of the domestic, producing a miniature leopard with a loving nature. The appearance of the Bengal should be as close as possible to that of the first cross, but without the possibility of its being mistaken for an actual Asian leopard cat. The texture of this breed's coat is unique, having the feel of satin or silk, and a glittering appearance as if sprinkled with gold dust or fragments of pearl.

Breakdown of 100 show points

- Coat   45 points
- Body   35 points
- Head   20 points

BROWN MARBLE TABBY BENGAL

Striking markings easily identify Bengals with the marble pattern, with its complex whorls, distinct shapes, and sharp outlines.

Key characteristics

Category Foreign shorthair.

Overall build Large.

Body Robust with a broad chest, very muscular, but long and sleek, with hindquarters slightly higher than the shoulders.

Colors Leopard spotted or marble markings in brown tabby, brown snow, blue-eyed snow, or blue.

Ears Medium to small, rather short with a wide base and rounded tips; set as much on the side as the top of the head; pointing forward in profile.

Head Broad, medium wedge with rounded contours, rather small in proportion to the body. Profile has a gentle curve from the forehead to the bridge of the nose; prominent brow.

Tail Of medium length, thick and even with a rounded tip.

Eyes Oval or slightly almond-shaped, large but not bold, set on the slant toward base of ear.

Coat Short to medium length, dense, luxuriant and unusually soft to touch.

Nose Large, broad nose with a puffed nose leather. Full broad muzzle and pronounced whisker pads.

Chin Strong.

Legs Medium length, strong and muscular.

Paws Large and rounded.

Penalties given for

- Long, rough, or coarse coat
- Ticked coat
- Incorrect color of the tail tip or paw pads
- Whip tail
- Unspotted stomach
- White patches or spots other than the *ocelli* (light spots on the backs of the ears)

Disqualification features

- Aggressive behavior that threatens to harm

Its cooing or chirruping call is quite different from that of the ordinary domestic cat, which adds to the impression the ideal Bengal gives of being a truly wild cat.

Character and care

Self-assured and as confident as its leopard cat ancestors, the Bengal has acquired an affectionate disposition and a loving, dependable temperament.

The thick, luxuriant coat is kept in good condition with a well-balanced diet, and regular brushing and combing.

Bengal: TABBY & OTHER VARIETIES

*Marble and leopard spotted
tabbies are recognized.
The marble has large swirled
patches or streaks that give
it a marble-like impression
and bears no resemblance to
the classic tabby pattern.*

Brown tabby

- All variations are allowed, but a high degree of reddish brown yielding a yellow, buff, golden, or orange ground color is preferred. Markings may be black or shades of brown, and there may be *ocelli*. The whisker pads and chin must be very pale; the chest, underbody, and inner legs should be pale compared with the general ground color.
- Eye rims, lips, and nose leather are outlined in black; the center of the nose leather is brick red; paw pads and tail tip are black; eye color is gold, green, or hazel, with deep shades preferred.

Brown snow

- This variety shows the Burmese/ Tonkinese restriction of coat pattern, where the most intense color is at the points, but the pattern is still visible on the body and has a special glittering appearance. The ground color is cream to light brown; the pattern varies from charcoal to light brown. There are light-colored spectacles, whisker pads, and chin; *ocelli* are preferred on each ear.
- Eye rims, lips, and nose leather are outlined in black; the center of the nose leather is brick red; paw pads are rosy brown; tail tip is charcoal or dark brown; eye color is gold, green, or blue green.

Blue-eyed snow

- This variety is of the Himalayan type, with the pattern restricted to the points. The ground color is ivory to cream; the pattern varies from charcoal to dark or light brown. There are light-colored spectacles, whisker pads, and chin; *ocelli* are preferred on each ear.
- Eye rims, lips, and nose leather are outlined in black; the center of the nose leather is brick red; paw pads are rosy brown; tail tip is charcoal or dark brown; eye color is blue.

Blue

- The ground color is pinkish mushroom to warm oatmeal. The clearly visible pattern is pale blue to blue gray; there are light-colored spectacles, whisker pads, and chin; and *ocelli* are preferred on each ear.
- Eye rims, lips, and nose leather are outlined in slate gray; the center of the nose leather is dark pink; paw pads are mauvish pink; tail tip is dark blue; eye color is gold, green, or blue green.

Cornish Rex

In 1950 a curly coated kitten was born in an otherwise normal litter at a farm in Cornwall in southwestern England. Microscopic examination by a geneticist of the kitten's hair samples showed they were similar to those of the Rex rabbit. When the kitten, named Kallibunker, matured, he was mated with his mother, and two of the resulting three kittens had Rex coats. The male, Poldhu, eventually sired a stunning Rex female called Lamorna Cove, which was exported to the United States to found the Cornish Rex breed on that side of the Atlantic. British Shorthairs and Burmese cats were used as foundation stock in the early days of Cornish Rex breeding, and eventually there were enough curly coated cats to establish an acceptable breed that could be registered. The Cornish Rex achieved full breed status in the UK in 1967, and in the United States in 1979.

In order to widen the gene pool and to ensure stamina in the Cornish Rex as a breed, it was necessary for the pioneer breeders to outcross to other breeds having the desired conformation.

Breakdown of 100 show points

- Coat   35 points
- Body & legs   20 points
- Head   15 points
- Eyes   10 points
- Ears   10 points
- Whiskers & eyebrows 5 points
- Tail   5 points

RED CORNISH REX
The Cornish Rex is medium size, lithe, and muscular, with long slender legs and small oval paws.

Key characteristics

Category Foreign shorthair, curled.
Overall build Medium.
Body Slender, hard, and muscular.
Colors Most associations accept virtually all colors and patterns except white markings on Siamese-patterned cats.

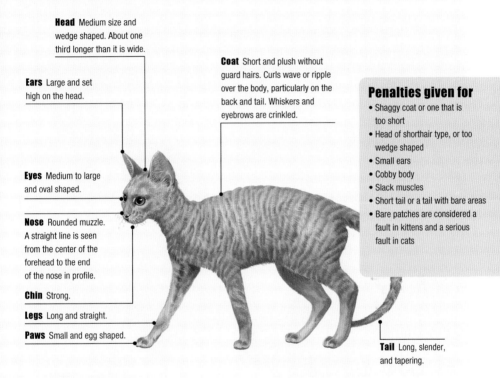

Head Medium size and wedge shaped. About one third longer than it is wide.

Coat Short and plush without guard hairs. Curls wave or ripple over the body, particularly on the back and tail. Whiskers and eyebrows are crinkled.

Ears Large and set high on the head.

Eyes Medium to large and oval shaped.

Nose Rounded muzzle. A straight line is seen from the center of the forehead to the end of the nose in profile.

Chin Strong.

Legs Long and straight.

Paws Small and egg shaped.

Tail Long, slender, and tapering.

Penalties given for

- Shaggy coat or one that is too short
- Head of shorthair type, or too wedge shaped
- Small ears
- Cobby body
- Slack muscles
- Short tail or a tail with bare areas
- Bare patches are considered a fault in kittens and a serious fault in cats

Foreign breeds were selected in the main, including chocolate and lilac Oriental Shorthairs, and Burmese as well as Siamese of various colors. All the offspring of Cornish Rex to non-Rex cats resulted in cats with normal coats, all carrying the recessive gene for the Cornish curly coat. When such cats matured and were mated with similar cats or back to Cornish Rex, curly coated kittens were produced.

Character and care

The Cornish Rex cat is intelligent, affectionate, and rather extrovert by nature. Playful and mischievous, it makes a wonderful pet.

The unique curled coat does not shed hair, making it extremely easy to groom with hand stroking and the occasional use of a comb.

Cornish Rex: COLOR VARIETIES

The various colors and coat patterns of the cats selected for the original outcross breeding resulted in a wide range of color varieties in the Cornish Rex, and breeders soon began to show their preferences for certain colors and combinations of colors.

BLACK SMOKE VAN PATTERN

Perhaps one of the most unusual of the Cornish Rex is the van pattern, in which the cat's coat is basically white, with color restricted to the extremities.

BLACK SMOKE & WHITE

The tail of the Cornish Rex is long, fine, and tapered, and must be well covered with waved fur.

CHOCOLATE SMOKE

The short plush coat is dense and has uniform narrow waves extending from the top of the head across the back, sides, and hips, and continuing to the tip of the tail.

WHITE
The head should be narrow with a flat skull. A straight line can be seen from the center of the forehead to the end of the nose.

CHOCOLATE TORTIE
The eyes of the Cornish Rex are medium size and oval, with a full eye's width between them.

TORTIE SMOKE & WHITE
The Cornish Rex stands tall, appearing to walk on tiptoe.

Devon Rex

Ten years after the discovery of the first Cornish Rex kitten, another curly coated kitten was discovered in the neighboring English county of Devon. The kitten, named Kirlee, was eventually mated with some Cornish Rex queens. To everyone's surprise, all the resulting kittens were flat coated, and it was concluded that Kirlee's curls were caused by a different gene. More breeding tests confirmed this. The gene for the Cornish coat was labeled Rex gene [i]; the gene for the Devon coat Rex gene [ii]. The two Rex-coated varieties were developed separately and are quite distinct breeds.

The Devon Rex would look rather unusual even without its wavy coat, having a quizzical, pixie-like expression and huge, bat-like ears.

Like the Cornish Rex, the first Devons were outcrossed to cats of other foreign breeds in order to widen the gene pool of available breeding stock. Siamese cats were extensively used, and the resulting curled cats were called Si-Rex in the

TORBIE & WHITE DEVON REX
Tortoiseshells of all colors may have white markings and can be very bright and attractive, like this alert young cat.

Breakdown of 100 show points

• Coat	40 points
• Body, legs, & neck	25 points
• Head	15 points
• Ears	10 points
• Eyes	5 points
• Tail	5 points

Key characteristics

Category Foreign shorthair, curled.
Overall build Medium.
Body Hard, muscular, straight, and slender, but with a broad chest.
Colors All recognized colors or patterns except white markings on Siamese-patterned cats.

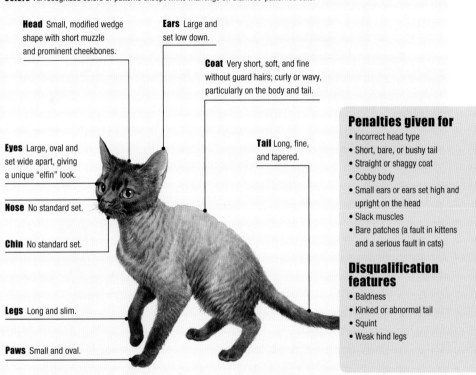

Head Small, modified wedge shape with short muzzle and prominent cheekbones.

Ears Large and set low down.

Coat Very short, soft, and fine without guard hairs; curly or wavy, particularly on the body and tail.

Eyes Large, oval and set wide apart, giving a unique "elfin" look.

Tail Long, fine, and tapered.

Nose No standard set.

Chin No standard set.

Legs Long and slim.

Paws Small and oval.

Penalties given for

- Incorrect head type
- Short, bare, or bushy tail
- Straight or shaggy coat
- Cobby body
- Small ears or ears set high and upright on the head
- Slack muscles
- Bare patches (a fault in kittens and a serious fault in cats)

Disqualification features

- Baldness
- Kinked or abnormal tail
- Squint
- Weak hind legs

beginning. Si-Rex is not now accepted as correct terminology for the Siamese-patterned Devon Rex, and white markings are not permitted in cats with the Himalayan or Siamese coat pattern, where the color is restricted to the cat's points.

Character and care

The Devon is said to be the cat for the connoisseur. It is demanding as a pet, constantly craving human attention, loving, playful, and intelligent.

The cat is very easy to groom with hand stroking and occasional combing. It often shows sparse areas on the body, and when it does, the cat needs extra warmth. The large ears need regular cleaning.

Devon Rex: COLOR VARIETIES

All colors and patterns accepted in the feline standards are recognized in the Devon Rex, which must conform to the same stringent show standard of points.

ODD-EYED WHITE
White Devon Rex cats are accepted with blue eyes, golden eyes, or odd eyes.

BLACK SMOKE
The Devon Rex is totally different from the Cornish. It is of similar size, but has a unique head type and unusual body conformation.

TORBIE

All feline colors are accepted in this breed, though some associations disallow any white markings except in tortoiseshell varieties.

CHOCOLATE TORTIE POINT

The Devon Rex appears in a range of Siamese-patterned colors. At one time these cats were called Si-Rex.

LILAC POINT

Siamese patterns are quite usual, but the eye color is generally paler in the Rex breeds than in the true Siamese.

Sphynx

Although it appears so, the Sphynx is not truly hairless. The skin has the texture of soft leather and may be covered with a fine down that is almost imperceptible to the eye. A fine covering of hair is sometimes apparent on the ears, muzzle, feet, tail, and scrotum.

The first Sphynx appeared as a spontaneous mutation in a litter born to a black and white domestic cat in Ontario, Canada, in 1966. A breeder of Siamese cats took the hairless kitten, and with other breeders worked on the development of a new breed. The CFA gave the Sphynx provisional status, then revoked it. The CCFF recognized the breed for championship status in 1971, and the first champion was chosen in 1972. Today the Sphynx is accepted only by a few feline associations, and it remains a rare and unique breed.

BLACK & WHITE SPHYNX

The Sphynx may appear to be hairless but is usually covered with a very short, fine down. The head is a modified wedge shape with rounded contours.

Breakdown of 100 show points

- Head — 35 points
- Body — 35 points
- Coat & skin — 25 points
- Color — 5 points

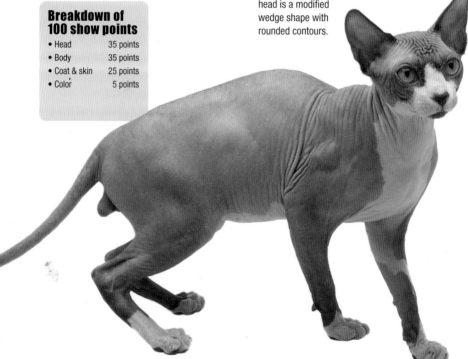

Key characteristics

Category Foreign.
Overall build Medium.
Body Hard and muscular, with a broad chest and well-rounded abdomen.
Colors All colors and patterns are acceptable; white lockets and buttons are also accepted.

Head Medium-sized, modified wedge, with rounded contours. Skull is slightly rounded, forehead is flat, and cheekbones are prominent.

Ears Broad based and very open, set upright on the head, hairless inside, and slightly haired on the back.

Coat Appears hairless; may be covered with short, fine down. Kittens have wrinkled skin; adults should retain some wrinkles.

Tail Whip-like, tapering from the body to the tip. A lion tail (with a tuft of hair on the tip) is acceptable.

Nose Slight stop at the bridge of the nose, and the muzzle is rounded, with a distinct whisker break.

Eyes Large and almost round, slanting toward the outer corner of the ear.

Chin Firm.

Legs In proportion to the body and of medium bone; hind legs longer than forelegs, which are wide set and muscular.

Paws Medium size, oval, with long, slender toes and thick paw pads.

Penalties given for
- Being overall a small cat
- Body that is too thin or frail in appearance
- Too fine boned, too cobby, or foreign in type
- Lack of wrinkles on the head
- Straight profile
- Narrow head
- Non-amenable disposition
- Significant amount of hair anywhere above the ankle
- Any indication of removal of hair

Character and care

People-orientated and not fond of other cats, the Sphynx does not like being held or strongly petted. It often stands with one foreleg raised, and resists lying with its body touching the ground, preferring a warm surface.

It never needs brushing, but the suede-like body must be kept in good condition by hand grooming and rubbing down with a soft cloth.

Japanese Bobtail

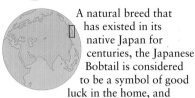

A natural breed that has existed in its native Japan for centuries, the Japanese Bobtail is considered to be a symbol of good luck in the home, and the tricolored variety, known as the Mi-Ke (meaning three colors), is particularly favored.

The Bobtail first came to the attention of cat fanciers in the Western world when an American cat show judge visiting Japan became captivated by the breed.

Five years later, in 1968, three Bobtails were exported from Japan to the United States. More were to follow, and Bobtails were accepted for provisional status by the CFA in May 1971.

After five years of careful breeding, the Japanese Bobtail became well

Breakdown of 100 show points

• Type	30 points
• Head	20 points
• Color & markings	20 points
• Tail	20 points
• Coat	10 points

BLACK & WHITE VAN PATTERN JAPANESE BOBTAIL
The unique tail of the Bobtail is short and may be straight or bent into one or more curves, with the hair fanning out to create a pompom effect. In the van pattern, the coat is white with color restricted to the extremities.

Key characteristics

Category Shorthair.
Overall build Medium.
Body Lean and well muscled.
Colors White, black, red, black and white, red and white, *Mi-Ke* (tricolor black, red, and white), tortoiseshell. Other colors include any other color or pattern or combination of colors and patterns except coloring that is restricted to the points, such as Himalayan, or unpatterned agouti, such as Abyssinian ticking. Patterned categories include any variety of tabby with or without areas of solid unmarked color, preference being given to bold, dramatic markings and rich, vivid coloring.

Head Long and fine, forming a perfect equilateral triangle with gentle curving lines, high cheek bones, and a noticeable whisker break.

Ears Large and upright, set wide apart, and at right angles to the head.

Eyes Large, oval, wide and alert.

Nose The muzzle is fairly broad, rounding into the whisker break.

Chin Medium.

Legs Long and slender.

Paws Neat and oval.

Coat Soft, silky, and medium length; no noticeable undercoat and relatively little shedding of hair.

Tail Short and said to resemble a bunny tail with the hair fanning out to create a pompom effect. If straightened, the tail bone could be four or five inches in length. It is usually jointed only at the base and may be either straight or composed of one or more curves and angles.

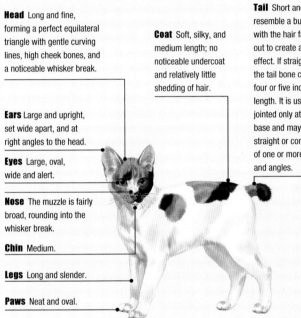

Penalties given for
- Short, round head
- Cobby build

Disqualification features
- Tail bone absent or extending too far beyond the body
- Tail bone lacking a pompom or a fluffy appearance
- The delayed pompom effect, apparent when the pompom is preceded by an inch or two of normal tail with close-lying fur, rather than appearing to start at the base of the spine

established in the United States and gained full recognition and championship status in the CFA in May 1976. It is also recognized in the UK by the Cat Association.

Character and care

The Japanese Bobtail has an endearing personality and loves human company. It is a vocal cat, and has a soft, melodious voice with a range of sounds. As a house cat, the Bobtail is well behaved, intelligent, and playful; and as a show cat it is easy to handle.

The silky coat is easy to maintain in perfect condition with gentle brushing and combing, finishing with the hands or a silk scarf. The pompom on the tail is combed into shape, and the wide ears are kept in pristine condition by wiping daily with a cotton swab.

Burmese

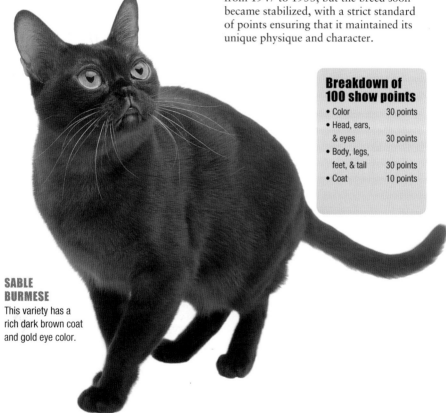

All modern Burmese cats can trace their ancestry back to a Siamese hybrid female named Wong Mau, who was taken from Rangoon to the United States in 1930. Wong Mau was almost certainly a cat of the type known as Tonkinese today. At first she was mated with Siamese males; then her offspring were intermated, and some backcrossed to Wong Mau herself.

From these matings three distinct types of kittens emerged—some identical to Wong Mau, some Siamese, and some much darker than Wong Mau. These latter cats were the foundation of the Burmese breed, which was officially recognized in 1936 by the Cat Fanciers' Association, and was the first breed of pedigree cats to be developed completely in the US.

Due to the lack of suitable Burmese cats, outcrosses to Siamese were made from time to time. Because of this, registration was suspended by the CFA from 1947 to 1953, but the breed soon became stabilized, with a strict standard of points ensuring that it maintained its unique physique and character.

Breakdown of 100 show points

• Color	30 points
• Head, ears, & eyes	30 points
• Body, legs, feet, & tail	30 points
• Coat	10 points

SABLE BURMESE

This variety has a rich dark brown coat and gold eye color.

Key characteristics

Category Foreign shorthair.

Overall build Medium, but surprisingly heavy.

Body Muscular and compact, with strong shoulders and hips, and substantial bone structure.

Colors In some US associations, only the sable (brown) varieties are classed as Burmese. The blue, champagne (chocolate), and platinum (lilac) are classed as dilute division Burmese in some associations, and as Malayan in others. In the UK, red, cream, tortie, and pointed varieties are also accepted, and all colors compete as Burmese.

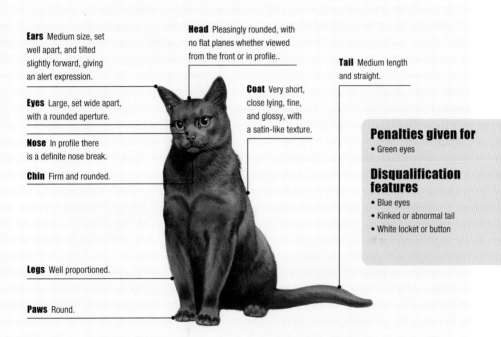

Ears Medium size, set well apart, and tilted slightly forward, giving an alert expression.

Eyes Large, set wide apart, with a rounded aperture.

Nose In profile there is a definite nose break.

Chin Firm and rounded.

Legs Well proportioned.

Paws Round.

Head Pleasingly rounded, with no flat planes whether viewed from the front or in profile..

Coat Very short, close lying, fine, and glossy, with a satin-like texture.

Tail Medium length and straight.

Penalties given for
- Green eyes

Disqualification features
- Blue eyes
- Kinked or abnormal tail
- White locket or button

Burmese cats were exported to the UK and accepted at shows during the 1950s. Since then, the breed has developed to slightly different standards on opposite sides of the Atlantic. The American Burmese has a rounder head and a slightly heavier body than its British counterpart. American Burmese also tend to have better eye color.

Character and care

The Burmese is a highly intelligent, active cat that can be strong willed, but repays firm, kind handling with affection.

Its short, glossy coat needs very little grooming to keep it in top condition.

Burmese: SOLID VARIETIES

There are some differences in color terminology. Sable, champagne, and platinum are used in the US; in the UK these colors are referred to as brown, chocolate, and lilac respectively.

Red

- The coat is a light tangerine color and as even as possible, though very slight tabby markings are allowed on the face. The ears are darker than the body.
- Nose leather and paw pads are pink; eye color is yellow to gold, with deeper shades preferred.

Cream

- The coat is pastel cream, with ears slightly darker than the body. The paler colors often show a very slight Himalayan effect, with darker color on the points.
- Nose leather and paw pads are pink; eye color is yellow to gold, with deeper shapes preferred.

Sable

- The rich, dark brown coat graduates almost imperceptibly to a lighter tone on the underparts, without any shading, barring, or markings of any kind. Kittens may be lighter in color.
- Nose leather and paw pads are brown; eye color ranges from yellow to gold, with deeper shades preferred.

Blue

- A simple dilute of the usual brown color, the blue has a soft, silver gray coat that is slightly darker on the back and tail. There should be a distinct silver sheen on the ears, face, and feet.
- Nose leather and paw pads are blue gray; eye color is yellow to gold.

Platinum

- The pale delicate dove gray coat has a pinkish tone. It should be as even as possible, though the mask and ears may be very slightly deeper in color.
- Nose leather and paw pads are lavender pink; eye color is yellow to gold, with deeper shades preferred.

Champagne

- The warm milk chocolate coat should be as even as possible, though the mask and ears may be very slightly deeper in color.
- Nose leather is chocolate brown; paw pads are cinnamon to chocolate brown; eye color is yellow to gold, with deeper shades preferred.

Burmese: TORTOISESHELL & POINTED VARIETIES

The red/orange gene was introduced into the Burmese from three sources: a shorthaired ginger tabby, a red-pointed Siamese, and a calico domestic cat. As well as resulting in the solid red Burmese and cream Burmese (see page 170), tortoiseshells were also produced.

Blue tortie

- The coat is pale blue patched and/or mottled with cream.
- Nose leather and paw pads are plain or mottled pink and/or blue gray; eye color is yellow to gold, with deeper shades preferred.

Seal tortie

- The coat is seal brown patched and/or mottled with red and/or light red.
- Nose leather and paw pads are plain or mottled seal brown and/or pink; eye color is yellow to gold, with deeper shades preferred.

Lilac tortie

- The coat is lilac patched and/or mottled with pale cream.
- Nose leather and paw pads are plain or mottled pale pink and/or lavender pink; eye color is yellow to gold, with deeper shades preferred.

Chocolate tortie

- The coat is milk chocolate patched and/or mottled with red and/or light red.
- Nose leather and paw pads are plain or mottled milk chocolate and/or light red or pink; eye color is yellow to gold, with deeper shades preferred.

Pointed

- The points—mask, ears, legs and paws, and tail—are the same as the body color, showing little contrast, but should be as equal in color density as possible. In all varieties, the body color will be paler on the underparts than on the back and legs.
- The eye color is in the yellow/gold range, with deeper shades preferred.

Singapura

In its native Singapore, this breed is referred to as the Drain Cat, a name that reflects both its lifestyle and the low esteem in which cats are held by the residents there. As a result, Singapore's native street cats have led deprived lives for generations, roaming the streets wild and often seeking shelter in drains. The lifestyle is a probable cause of their smaller bodies, in comparison with those of other oriental breeds.

An American cat breeder, Tommy Meadows, imported some Singapuras into the United States, and drew up a careful program for the development of the breed. Her work has been rewarded by the production of an attractive, viable feline breed with considerable esthetic appeal. The Singapura has a ticked coat, similar to that of the Abyssinian, and is of moderate foreign shorthair bone structure and conformation.

Breakdown of 100 show points

- Color &
  markings   30 points
- Body, legs,
  & tail   20 points
- Coat   15 points
- Head   15 points
- Ears   10 points
- Eyes   10 points

SINGAPURA

With its short, fine ticked coat and happy, friendly nature, this rare breed makes a perfect pet.

Key characteristics

Category Foreign shorthair.

Overall build Small to medium.

Body Moderately stocky and muscular.

Colors Sepia agouti: ground color is warm ivory; ticking is dark brown; muzzle, chin, chest, and stomach are the color of unbleached muslin; ears and bridge of the nose are salmon toned; nose leather is pale to dark salmon pink, outlined with dark brown; paw pads are rosy brown; eye rims are dark brown; eye color is hazel, green, or yellow.

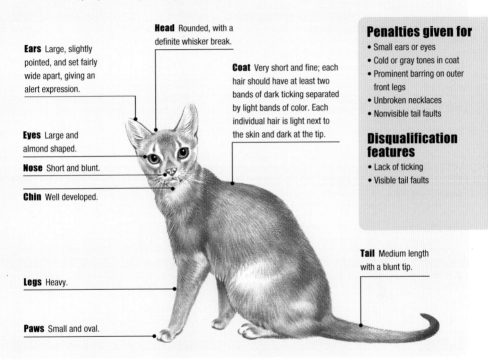

Head Rounded, with a definite whisker break.

Ears Large, slightly pointed, and set fairly wide apart, giving an alert expression.

Coat Very short and fine; each hair should have at least two bands of dark ticking separated by light bands of color. Each individual hair is light next to the skin and dark at the tip.

Eyes Large and almond shaped.

Nose Short and blunt.

Chin Well developed.

Legs Heavy.

Paws Small and oval.

Tail Medium length with a blunt tip.

Penalties given for

- Small ears or eyes
- Cold or gray tones in coat
- Prominent barring on outer front legs
- Unbroken necklaces
- Nonvisible tail faults

Disqualification features

- Lack of ticking
- Visible tail faults

Character and care

The Singapura is a happy, friendly cat with a playful nature. Its street ancestry has equipped the animal to adapt quickly and easily to whatever situation it finds itself in, but it prefers a peaceful, indoor existence.

The short, fine coat is extremely easy to keep in good condition with very little grooming. A light combing removes dead hairs, and occasional brushing tones the skin. Hand grooming or stroking with a silk scarf imparts a healthy looking sheen to the coat.

Tonkinese

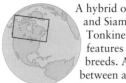

A hybrid of Burmese and Siamese cats, the Tonkinese has physical features of both these breeds. A mating between a Burmese and a Siamese produces all Tonkinese kittens, whereas the mating of two Tonkinese cats produces, on average, two Tonkinese kittens to one Burmese and one Siamese.

Tonkinese cats have dark points that merge gradually into the body color, which is intermediate between the typical pale Siamese and the dark Burmese coloring. Tonkinese eye color is blue green or turquoise, never Siamese blue or Burmese gold.

Breakdown of 100 show points

- Coat pattern
  & color   20 points
- Head   15 points
- Body   15 points
- Eye color   10 points
- Coat texture   10 points
- Temperament   10 points
- Tail   5 points
- Legs & paws   5 points
- Ears   5 points
- Eye shape   5 points

CHOCOLATE TORTIE TONKINESE
The introduction of the red/orange gene into Tonkinese breeding soon gave rise to an entire range of tortoiseshells.

Key characteristics

Category Foreign shorthair.

Overall build Medium, but surprisingly heavy.

Body Muscular but not coarse, with a tight abdomen.

Colors In the US: natural (brown) mink, blue mink, champagne (chocolate) mink, platinum (lilac) mink, honey (red) mink. In the UK: all accepted Burmese colors, including tortie, tabby, and torbie patterns.

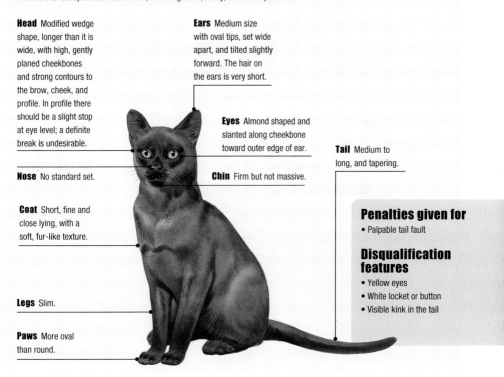

Head Modified wedge shape, longer than it is wide, with high, gently planed cheekbones and strong contours to the brow, cheek, and profile. In profile there should be a slight stop at eye level; a definite break is undesirable.

Ears Medium size with oval tips, set wide apart, and tilted slightly forward. The hair on the ears is very short.

Eyes Almond shaped and slanted along cheekbone toward outer edge of ear.

Tail Medium to long, and tapering.

Nose No standard set.

Chin Firm but not massive.

Coat Short, fine and close lying, with a soft, fur-like texture.

Legs Slim.

Paws More oval than round.

Penalties given for
• Palpable tail fault

Disqualification features
• Yellow eyes
• White locket or button
• Visible kink in the tail

Character and care

The Tonkinese is a friendly and affectionate cat, with a strong sense of mischief. Extrovert and intelligent, it is generally good with other cats, as well as with dogs and children. It is less vocal than the Siamese.

The coat is easy to keep in good condition with very little grooming. Regular combing to remove dead hair and buffing with a silk scarf or grooming mitt imparts a healthy sheen.

Tonkinese: MINK & POINTED VARIETIES

The name mink is used because of the Tonkinese's soft, dense, lustrous fur. The colors natural, champagne, platinum, and honey may also be referred to as brown, chocolate, lilac, and red respectively.

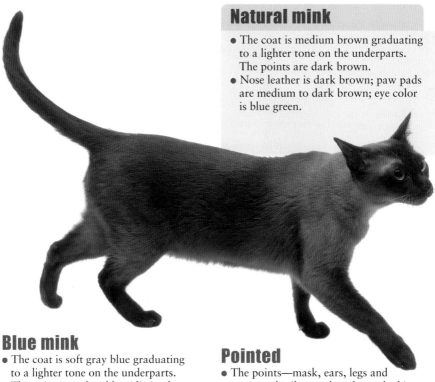

Natural mink

- The coat is medium brown graduating to a lighter tone on the underparts. The points are dark brown.
- Nose leather is dark brown; paw pads are medium to dark brown; eye color is blue green.

Blue mink

- The coat is soft gray blue graduating to a lighter tone on the underparts. The points are slate blue (distinctly darker than the body color).
- Nose leather and paw pads are blue gray; eye color is blue green.

Honey mink

- The coat is golden cream graduating to apricot underparts. The points are light to medium ruddy brown.
- Nose leather and paw pads are caramel pink; eye color is blue green.

Pointed

- The points—mask, ears, legs and paws, and tail—are densely marked in a darker shade of the body color, and gradually merge into the body color. There is a distinct contrast between the points and body color whatever the color variety. The body color should be rich and even, graduating almost imperceptibly into a slightly lighter color on the underparts.
- Eye color is deep, clear, brilliant blue green.

Champagne mink

- The coat is buff cream; the points are medium brown.
- Nose leather is cinnamon brown; paw pads are cinnamon pink to cinnamon brown; eye color is blue green.

Platinum mink

- The coat is pale silvery gray with warm overtones (not white or cream). The points are pewter gray, distinctly darker than the body color.
- Nose leather is lavender pink to lavender gray; paw pads are lavender pink; eye color is blue green.

Tonkinese: NEW VARIETIES

The Cat Association of Britain offers special awards for Tonkinese in the following color varieties: seal, blue, chocolate, cinnamon, lilac, fawn, caramel, beige, red, cream, apricot, indigo, and all these colors as tortoiseshell, tabby, and torbie.

RED
Red Tonkinese are often quite similar to cream Tonkinese and can be difficult to tell apart as kittens.

CREAM
This cat is a rich, warm cream with slightly darker points, except for the legs, which may be paler than in other colors.

BLUE TORTIE
Bluish silver gray
either patched or
mingled with shades
of cream produce
this pretty variety.

LILAC TORTIE
The lilac tortie is a
paler version of the
blue tortie, with pale
dove gray patched
or mingled with pale
cream. Like its darker
cousin, the lilac tortie
has blue green eyes.

Bombay

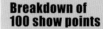

Because of its looks, the Bombay cat has been referred to as the "patent-leather kid with new-penny eyes," an apt description for this shining jet black feline. Developed from outstanding specimens of black American Shorthair and sable Burmese, the desired type was quickly achieved, and Bombays were found to breed true. Full recognition and championship status was granted by the CFA in 1976.

Breakdown of 100 show points

- Color   30 points
- Head & ears   25 points
- Body   20 points
- Coat   20 points
- Eyes   5 points

BOMBAY

The true Bombay was produced from sable Burmese and black American Shorthairs. It is a unique jet black and shiny cat with large golden eyes.

Category Foreign shorthair.
Overall build Medium, but surprisingly heavy.
Body Muscular, with legs in proportion.
Colors Black only. The coat is jet black to the roots with a patent-leather sheen; nose leather and paw pads are black; eye color is gold to copper, with deeper shades preferred.

Ears Medium size with slightly rounded tips set wide apart and tilting slightly forward, giving an alert expression.

Head Pleasingly round head with no sharp angles, full face with good width between the eyes, tapering to a short, strong muzzle.

Coat Fine and short with satin-like texture, close lying, and with a sheen like patent leather.

Eyes Round.

Nose In profile there is a visible nose break.

Chin Strong.

Legs Medium length.

Paws Round.

Tail Straight and medium length.

Penalties given for
- Excessive cobbiness or ranginess

Disqualification features
- Incorrect color of nose leather, paw pads, or eyes
- Incorrect dentition
- Kinked or abnormal tail
- White locket or spots
- Extreme nose break interfering with normal breathing or tear production

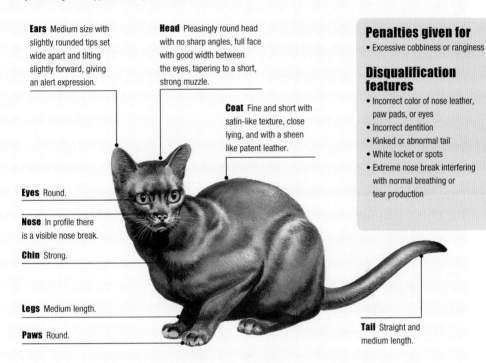

Although the cat looks like a black American-style Burmese, the early pioneers of the breed thought it looked like a miniature version of the Indian (Asian) black panther and so, after much deliberation, chose Bombay as the breed name.

Character and care
The Bombay has a very even temperament. It is generally strong, healthy, affectionate, and playful, making it a good pet.

The coat is easy to maintain with a balanced diet and minimal grooming. Buffing with a silk scarf or velvet grooming mitt enhances the typical patent-leather gloss.

Burmilla

An accidental mating between a lilac Burmese female and a chinchilla silver Persian male in 1981 resulted in the birth of four black-shaded silver female kittens. All were of foreign conformation and had short, dense coats. They looked so spectacular and caused so much interest that similar matings were carried out. In 1983, the Cat Association of Britain accepted breeding programs and a standard of points for the breed to be known as Burmilla, to be developed as a shorthaired silver cat of medium foreign type, showing a striking contrast between the pure silver undercoat and the shaded or tipped markings. FIFe granted international breed status to the Burmilla in 1994.

This elegant cat is of medium foreign type with a muscular body, long sturdy legs, and a moderately thick, long tail. The head is a medium wedge, with large ears, a short nose, and large expressive eyes. Its most impressive feature, however, is the sparkling shaded or tipped ("shell") coat. The ground color is pure silver white, with shading or tipping in any of the recognized solid or tortoiseshell

BLACK SHADED BURMILLA
As in all Burmilla cats, the paw pads match the color of the shading or tipping on the silver coat.

Breakdown of 100 show points

• Head	50 points
• Body	25 points
• Coat	20 points
• Condition	5 points

Key characteristics

Category Foreign shorthair.
Overall build Medium.
Body Straight back and rounded chest.
Colors Shaded or tipped in the following colors: black, blue, brown, chocolate, lilac, red, cream, red tortoiseshell, blue tortoiseshell, brown tortoiseshell, chocolate tortoiseshell, lilac tortoiseshell.

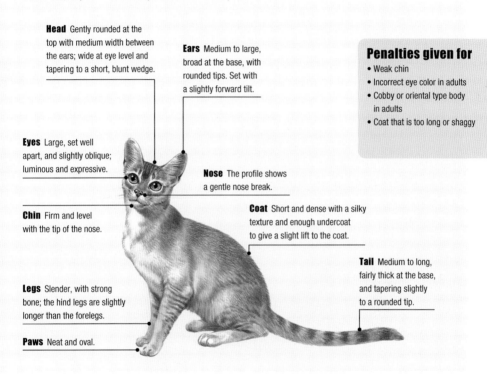

Head Gently rounded at the top with medium width between the ears; wide at eye level and tapering to a short, blunt wedge.

Ears Medium to large, broad at the base, with rounded tips. Set with a slightly forward tilt.

Eyes Large, set well apart, and slightly oblique; luminous and expressive.

Nose The profile shows a gentle nose break.

Chin Firm and level with the tip of the nose.

Coat Short and dense with a silky texture and enough undercoat to give a slight lift to the coat.

Tail Medium to long, fairly thick at the base, and tapering slightly to a rounded tip.

Legs Slender, with strong bone; the hind legs are slightly longer than the forelegs.

Paws Neat and oval.

Penalties given for
- Weak chin
- Incorrect eye color in adults
- Cobby or oriental type body in adults
- Coat that is too long or shaggy

colors, which must be uniformly distributed. The eyelids, lips, and nose leather are rimmed with the basic color, and delicate tracings of tabby markings are present on the points, which are more clearly defined on the shaded Burmilla than on the tipped varieties.

Character and care

The Burmilla is an easy-going and relaxed cat. It has a playful nature and is very affectionate.

The dense coat is best groomed with a rubber brush to loosen dead hairs before being given a thorough combing.

Burmilla: SHADED & TIPPED VARIETIES

Elegant cats of medium foreign conformation, the Burmilla male is larger and more stocky than the dainty female. In all colors, the tipped Burmilla is lighter overall than the shaded Burmilla.

Black

- The coat is pure silver white, shaded or tipped with black.
- Nose leather is brick red; paw pads and soles are black; eye color is green.

Chocolate

- The coat is pure silver white, shaded or tipped with milk chocolate.
- Nose leather is brick red; paw pads are chocolate tinged with pink; soles are chocolate; eye color is green.

Lilac

- The coat is pure silver white, shaded or tipped with lilac (light gray with a pinkish tinge).
- Nose leather is brick red; paw pads are lavender pink; soles are gray tinged with pink; eye color is green.

Red

- The coat is pure silver white, shaded or tipped with red.
- Nose leather and paw pads are pink; soles are red; eye color is green or amber.

Cream

- The coat is pure silver white, shaded or tipped with pale cream.
- Nose leather and paw pads are pink; soles are cream; eye color is green or amber.

Brown

- The coat is pure silver white, shaded or tipped with dark brown.
- Nose leather is brick red; paw pads and soles are dark brown; eye color is green.

Tortoiseshell

- The coat is pure white, shaded or tipped with a patchwork of colors: black and red in the red tortie; blue gray and cream in the blue tortie; dark brown and red or light red in the brown tortie; milk chocolate and light red in the chocolate tortie; and lilac and cream in the lilac tortie.
- Nose leather and paw pads are the main varietal color or pink, or mottled color/pink; eye color is green or amber.

Blue

- The coat is pure silver white, shaded or tipped with blue gray.
- Nose leather is brick red; paw pads and soles are blue gray; eye color is green.

Burmilla: OTHER ASIAN VARIETIES

The Burmilla is part of a larger family of cats known as the Asian group, most of which have arisen as off-shoots of the programs designed to breed the Burmilla. The group includes the Burmilla; solid, tabby, and smoke Asians; and the Tiffanie.

SOLID ASIAN
The black Asian is known as the Bombay in the UK; it should not be confused with the American Bombay (see page 182).

TABBY ASIAN
Each hair is ticked with two or three bands of color that produce the effect commonly seen in a wild rabbit. Clear tabby bars mark the legs and tail.

SHADED TIFFANIE

The Tiffanie is a semi-
longhaired product of
the Burmilla breeding
plan and is found in the
same range of shaded
and tipped colors.

SMOKE TIFFANIE

The Tiffanie combines
the conformation and
coloring of the Burmese
with a coat of long,
silky hair. It is found
in a range of smoke
colors, such as this
brown smoke Tiffanie.

Oriental
Breeds

Siamese

The Siamese cat of today is quite different from that seen in the early 1900s, though it still retains its points, caused by the Himalayan factor, the gene that restricts the true coloring to the animal's face, ears, legs, paws, and tail.

Seal-pointed cats were presented by the Royal Court of Siam to British and American diplomats toward the end of the nineteenth century. Although the original Royal Cats of Siam were seal-pointed, some had lighter brown points and were eventually recognized as being a separate color variety that was called chocolate point. A naturally occurring dilute factor also became apparent when the almost black coloration of the seal point gave rise to cats with slate gray extremities. These were eventually accepted as the color variety blue point.

Breeders of Siamese cats added the red series of point colors by outcrossing to red, red tabby, and tortoiseshell cats, and a range of colors in tabby-pointed cats was developed from outcrosses with tabbies.

Britain's GCCF and CA recognize all short-coated pointed cats of oriental type as Siamese, as do some foreign associations, in particular FIFe. Others, such as the United States' CFA, accept only the four original, naturally occurring colors as Siamese, and register the red series and tabby (or lynx point) series as Colorpoint Shorthairs.

CHOCOLATE POINT SIAMESE

The chocolate point has an ivory body and points of a warm milk chocolate.

Breakdown of 100 show points

- Head   15 points
- Body   15 points
- Body color   15 points
- Eye color   15 points
- Points color   10 points
- Coat texture   10 points
- Ears   5 points
- Eye shape
  & setting   5 points
- Tail   5 points
- Legs & feet   5 points

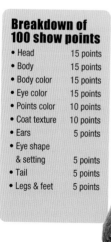

Key characteristics

Category Foreign shorthair.

Overall build Medium.

Body Long, svelte, and well muscled, but still dainty and elegant. The shoulders should not be wider than the hips.

Colors Seal point, blue point, chocolate point, lilac point, red point, cream point, seal tortie point, blue tortie point, chocolate tortie point, lilac tortie point, seal tabby point, blue tabby point, chocolate tabby point, lilac tabby point, red tabby point, cream tabby point, seal torbie point, blue torbie point, chocolate torbie point, lilac torbie point.

Head Medium size in proportion to the body; wedge shaped with straight lines, the wedge starting at the nose and gradually increasing in width in straight lines on each side to the ears. No whisker break.

Ears Large and pointed, wide at the base, placed to continue the line of the wedge-shaped head.

Eyes Medium size and almond shaped, set slightly slanting toward the nose in harmony with the lines of the wedge.

Coat Very short and fine, glossy, silky, and close lying.

Nose Long and straight without any break.

Chin Medium size, the tip forming a vertical line with the tip of the nose.

Tail Very long, thin at the base, and tapering to a fine point.

Legs Long and fine, in proportion to the body.

Paws Small and oval.

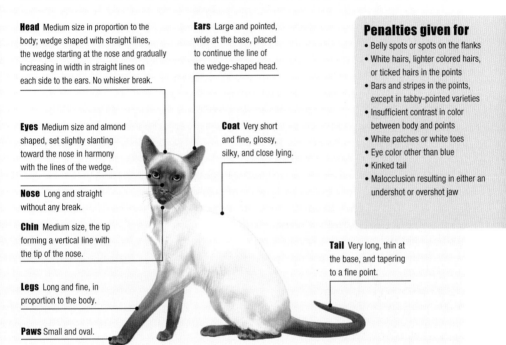

Penalties given for

- Belly spots or spots on the flanks
- White hairs, lighter colored hairs, or ticked hairs in the points
- Bars and stripes in the points, except in tabby-pointed varieties
- Insufficient contrast in color between body and points
- White patches or white toes
- Eye color other than blue
- Kinked tail
- Malocclusion resulting in either an undershot or overshot jaw

Character and care

The typical Siamese cat has an extrovert personality. It is very affectionate with people and pets that it likes, is lively and intelligent, and can be very vocal. Siamese cats do not like being left alone for long periods, and do better as pets when kept in pairs or small groups. They are naturally fastidiously clean and make perfect house pets.

The short, fine coat is kept in good condition by stroking with clean hands or buffing with a silk scarf. The large ears need regular cleaning, and Siamese should be provided with a scratching post and lots of toys.

Siamese: TABBY & OTHER VARIETIES

The body must be even in color, and the points—mask, ears, legs, paws, and tail—must be of the same shade and clearly defined. The eye color is deep, vivid blue.

Red point

- The body is creamy white; the points are bright, warm orange.
- Nose leather is pink; paw pads are pink and/or red.

Seal point

- The body is beige to cream or pale fawn; the points are dark seal brown.
- Nose leather and paw pads are dark seal brown.

Seal tabby point

- The body is beige; the points are dark seal tabby. The rims around the eyes and nose are seal brown.
- Nose leather is brick red, pink, or seal brown; paw pads are seal brown.

Seal tortie point

- The body is beige graduating to fawn; the points are seal patched or mingled with red and/or light red.
- Nose leather and paw pads are seal brown or pink.

Seal torbie point

- The body is beige; the points have seal tabby markings patched or mingled with red and/or light red tortie markings. The nose rims are seal.
- Nose leather and paw pads are seal, brick red, or pink, or seal mottled with brick red and/or pink.

Red tabby point

- The body is off-white with a slight red tinge; the points are warm orange tabby; the rims around the eyes and nose are dark pink.
- Nose leather is brick red or pink; paw pads are pink.

Cream point

- The body is creamy white; the points are a delicate pastel cream.
- Nose leather and paw pads are pink.

Chocolate point

- The body is ivory; the points are warm milk chocolate.
- Nose leather is milk chocolate; paw pads are cinnamon to milk chocolate.

Chocolate tabby point

- The body is ivory; the points are milk chocolate tabby. The rims around the eyes and nose are milk chocolate.
- Nose leather is light red, pink, or milk chocolate; paw pads are cinnamon to milk chocolate.

Chocolate tortie point

- The body is ivory; the points are milk chocolate patched or mingled with red and/or light red.
- Nose leather is milk chocolate and/or pink; paw pads are cinnamon to milk chocolate and/or pink.

Chocolate torbie point

- The body is ivory; the points have milk chocolate tabby markings patched or mingled with red and/or light red tortie markings. The nose rims are chocolate.
- Nose leather is milk chocolate, pale red, or pink, or milk chocolate mottled with pale red or pink; paw pads are cinnamon to milk chocolate and/or pink.

Cream tabby point

- The body is creamy white; the points are cream tabby with a cold tone; the rims around the eyes and nose are dark pink.
- Nose leather and paw pads are pink.

Siamese: TABBY & OTHER VARIETIES

continued

Blue point

- The body is bluish white of a glacial tone; the points are blue gray. Blue point Siamese often show more shading on the body than cats with other point colors.
- Nose leather and paw pads are blue gray.

Blue tabby point

- The body is bluish white; the points are blue gray tabby. The rims around the eyes and nose are blue gray.
- Nose leather is old rose or blue gray; paw pads are blue gray.

Blue torbie point

- The body is bluish white; the points have blue tabby markings patched or mingled with cream tortie markings. The nose rims are blue gray.
- Nose leather is blue gray, old rose, or pink, or blue gray mottled with old rose and/or pink; paw pads are blue gray and/or pink.

Blue tortie point

- The body is bluish white; the points are blue gray patched or mingled with pastel cream.
- Nose leather and paw pads are blue gray and/or pink.

Lilac point

- The body is glacial white; the points are frosty gray with a slight pinkish tone.
- Nose leather and paw pads are lavender pink.

Lilac tabby point

- The body is glacial white; the points are frosty gray with slightly pinkish tabby markings. The rims around the eyes and nose are lavender pink.
- Nose leather is lavender pink or pink; paw pads are lavender pink.

Lilac tortie point

- The body is glacial white; the points are frosty gray with a pinkish tone patched or mingled with pale cream.
- Nose leather and paw pads lavender pink and/or pale pink.

Lilac torbie point

- The body is glacial white; the points are frosty gray with slightly pinkish tabby markings patched or mingled with pale cream tortie markings. The nose rims are lavender pink.
- Nose leather and paw pads are lavender pink, pale pink, or lavender pink mottled with pale pink.

Colorpoint Shorthair

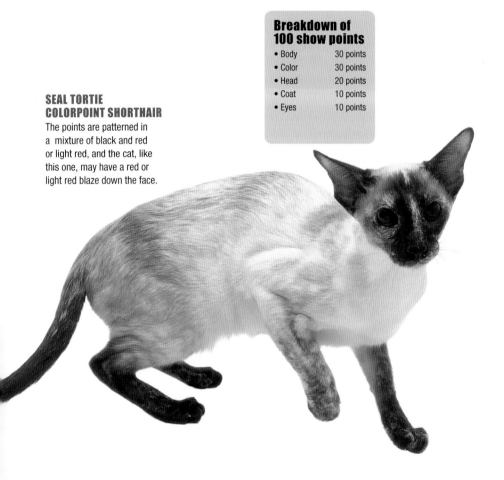

When Siamese cats were mated with cats of other varieties, such as the tabby shorthair, in order to achieve new colors and patterns, the Colorpoint Shorthair was the result. As the gene that restricts the color to the points in Siamese is recessive, the resulting kittens were colored all over.

When these crossbred cats were mated back to high-quality Siamese, however, Siamese-patterned offspring were produced, and successive backcrossing to Siamese upgraded the "new" Siamese to conform to the rigorous standards set by various associations. In the UK, the new colors were gradually

Breakdown of 100 show points
- Body — 30 points
- Color — 30 points
- Head — 20 points
- Coat — 10 points
- Eyes — 10 points

SEAL TORTIE COLORPOINT SHORTHAIR
The points are patterned in a mixture of black and red or light red, and the cat, like this one, may have a red or light red blaze down the face.

Category Foreign shorthair.

Overall build Medium.

Body Long and slender, with fine bones, firm muscles, and a tight abdomen. Slim shoulders and hips.

Colors Red point, cream point, seal lynx point, chocolate lynx point, blue lynx point, lilac lynx point, red lynx point, seal torbie point, chocolate torbie point, blue tortie point, lilac tortie point.

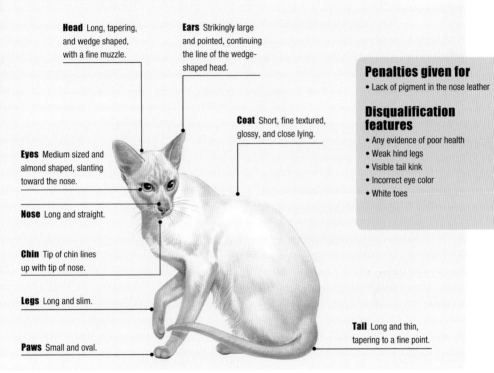

Head Long, tapering, and wedge shaped, with a fine muzzle.

Ears Strikingly large and pointed, continuing the line of the wedge-shaped head.

Coat Short, fine textured, glossy, and close lying.

Eyes Medium sized and almond shaped, slanting toward the nose.

Nose Long and straight.

Chin Tip of chin lines up with tip of nose.

Legs Long and slim.

Paws Small and oval.

Tail Long and thin, tapering to a fine point.

Penalties given for

- Lack of pigment in the nose leather

Disqualification features

- Any evidence of poor health
- Weak hind legs
- Visible tail kink
- Incorrect eye color
- White toes

accepted as additions to the Siamese varieties, but in the United States, some associations decided to accept such cats as Colorpoint Shorthairs.

Character and care

Siamese in everything but name, the Colorpoint Shorthair is a delightfully agile and affectionate pet.

It is very easy to maintain in top condition by feeding a good diet and needs minimal grooming: just combing through to remove any dead hair and buffing the fine coat either with the hands or a silk scarf.

Colorpoint Shorthair: COLOR VARIETIES

The eye color of all the following varieties is deep, vivid blue. On the lynx points, ghost striping is allowed as body shading, and the ears are the point color with a paler thumbprint in the center.

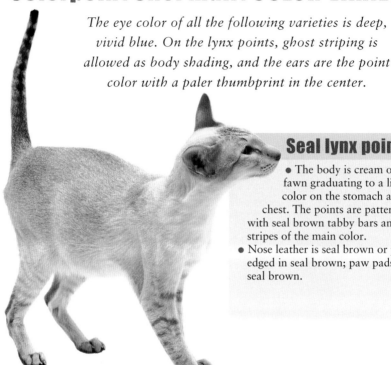

Seal lynx point

- The body is cream or pale fawn graduating to a lighter color on the stomach and chest. The points are patterned with seal brown tabby bars and stripes of the main color.
- Nose leather is seal brown or pink edged in seal brown; paw pads are seal brown.

Red point

- The body is clear white with any shading toning with the points, which should be bright apricot to deep red with no barring.
- Nose leather and paw pads are flesh or coral pink.

Cream point

- The body is clear white with any shading toning with the points, which should be pale buff to light pinkish cream with no barring.
- Nose leather and paw pads are flesh or coral pink.

Blue lynx point

- The body is bluish white to platinum gray graduating to a lighter color on the stomach and chest. The points are patterned with deep blue gray tabby bars and stripes of the main color.
- Nose leather is slate or pink edged with slate; paw pads are slate.

Chocolate lynx point

- The body is ivory. The points are patterned with warm milk chocolate tabby bars and stripes of the main color.
- Nose leather is cinnamon or pink edged in cinnamon; paw pads are cinnamon.

Chocolate tortie point

- The body is ivory and may be mottled in older cats. The points are warm milk chocolate uniformly mottled with red and/or light red. A blaze is desirable.
- Nose leather is cinnamon; flesh or coral mottling is permitted where there is a facial blaze. Paw pads are cinnamon; flesh or coral mottling is permitted where the points color mottling extends into the paw pads.

Lilac lynx point

- The body is glacial white. The points are patterned with frosty gray tabby bars and stripes of the main color.
- Nose leather is lavender pink or gray edged with lavender pink; paw pads are lavender pink.

Red lynx point

- The body is white. The points are patterned with deep red tabby bars and stripes of the main color.
- Nose leather and paw pads are flesh or coral pink.

Seal tortie point

- The body is pale fawn to cream and may be mottled in older cats. The points are seal brown uniformly mottled with red and light red. A blaze is desirable.
- Nose leather and paw pads are seal brown; mottling is permitted as for the chocolate tortie point.

Blue tortie point

- The body is bluish white to platinum gray graduating to a lighter color on the stomach and chest. The body color is mottled in older cats. The points are deep blue gray uniformly mottled with cream. A blaze is desirable.
- Nose leather and paw pads are slate; mottling is permitted as for the chocolate tortie point.

Lilac tortie point

- The body is glacial white. The points are frosty gray with a pinkish tone uniformly mottled with pale cream. A blaze is desirable.
- Nose leather and paw pads are lavender pink; mottling is permitted as for the chocolate tortie point.

Balinese

The long-coated kittens that appeared from time to time in otherwise normal litters of Siamese cats were developed into the Balinese. At first such kittens were quickly discarded and sold as pets, but in the 1940s two breeders in New York and California began to work toward the development of a separate breed. The name was chosen because of the cats' gracefulness and svelte lines, reminiscent of the dancers on the island of Bali. The breed soon gained a lot of admirers, but it was not until 1970 that the CFA first recognized it and granted it championship status. The long coat is nothing like that of the Persian. It has no woolly undercoat and lies flat against the body.

Breakdown of 100 show points
- Color & coat   50 points
- Type   50 points

SEAL TABBY POINT BALINESE
This cat epitomizes the Balinese breed, conforming almost exactly to the standard of points.

Category Shorthair.

Overall build Medium.

Body Long, svelte, and well muscled, but still dainty. The shoulders should not be wider than the hips.

Colors All the colors found in the Siamese and Colorpoint Shorthairs: seal point, blue point, chocolate point, lilac point, red point, cream point, seal tortie point, blue tortie point, chocolate tortie point, lilac tortie point, seal tabby point, blue tabby point, chocolate tabby point, lilac tabby point, red tabby point, cream tabby point, seal torbie point, blue torbie point, chocolate torbie point, lilac torbie point. Some associations accept only seal point, blue point, chocolate point, and lilac point.

Head Medium size; a long tapering wedge shape that starts at the nose and gradually increases in width in straight lines on each side as far as the ears. No whisker break.

Ears Large and pointed, wide at the base, placed to continue the line of the wedge-shaped head.

Coat Fine and silky.

Tail Very long and thin, tapering to a fine point; the tail hair spreads out like a plume.

Nose Long and straight, continuing the line from the forehead without any break.

Eyes Medium size and almond shaped, set slightly slanted toward the nose.

Chin Medium size, forming a vertical line with the nose.

Legs Long and fine, in proportion to the body.

Paws Small, dainty, and oval.

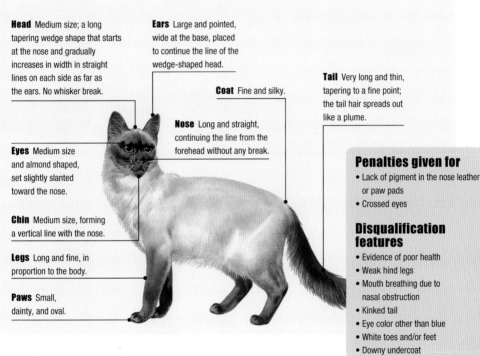

Penalties given for

- Lack of pigment in the nose leather or paw pads
- Crossed eyes

Disqualification features

- Evidence of poor health
- Weak hind legs
- Mouth breathing due to nasal obstruction
- Kinked tail
- Eye color other than blue
- White toes and/or feet
- Downy undercoat

Character and care

As might be expected from their ancestry, Balinese are very similar to Siamese in character—very affectionate, demanding of attention, extremely active, and highly inquisitive.

The coat is relatively easy to care for with regular gentle combing, and brushing of the ruff and plumed tail.

Balinese: TABBY & OTHER VARIETIES

The mask should cover the entire face, including the whisker pads, and be connected to the ears by traced markings. There should be no ticking or white hairs in the points. The eye color for all varieties is deep blue.

Blue point

- The body is bluish white of a glacial tone; the points are blue gray.
- Nose leather and paw pads are blue gray.

Seal point

- The body is beige to cream or pale fawn; the points are dark seal brown.
- Nose leather and paw pads are dark seal brown.

Chocolate point

- The body is ivory; the points are milk chocolate.
- Nose leather is milk chocolate; paw pads are cinnamon to milk chocolate.

Lilac point

- The body is glacial white; the points are frosty gray with a slight pinkish tone.
- Nose leather and paw pads are pink.

Red point

- The body is creamy white; the points are bright, warm orange.
- Nose leather is pink; paw pads are pink or red.

Tabby point

- There are six tabby point colors: seal, blue, chocolate, lilac, red, and cream. The body color is pale with the main varietal color as tabby markings on the points.
- Nose leather is red, pink, or the varietal color; paw pads are the varietal color or pink.

Cream point

- The body is creamy white; the points are pastel cream.
- Nose leather and paw pads are pink.

Torbie point

- Seal and chocolate torbie points have beige and ivory body colors respectively; the points have seal or milk chocolate tabby markings patched or mingled with red or light red tortie markings. The blue torbie point has a bluish white body color; the points have blue tabby markings patched or mingled with cream tortie markings. The lilac torbie point has a glacial white body color; the points have frosty gray tabby markings patched or mingled with pale cream tortie markings.
- Nose leather and paw pads are red, pink, or the main varietal color.

Tortie point

- There are four tortie point colors: seal, blue, chocolate, and lilac. The body color is pale; the points are the main varietal color patched or mingled with red and/or light red (chocolate and seal) or pale cream (blue and lilac).
- Nose leather and paw pads are the main varietal color and/or pink.

Oriental Shorthair

In the main, the Oriental Shorthair is identical to the Siamese in all respects except for not having its color restricted to the points and not having blue eyes. Oriental Shorthairs have been known for many years, but first became popular in the early 1960s when a small number of fanciers began to breed them in a wide variety of colors.

Britain's GCCF designates the solid-colored cats of Siamese type "Foreign," and so they are known as the Foreign White, Foreign Black, and so on. Europe's FIFe and its British member, the Cat Association of Britain, recognize the entire group as Oriental Shorthairs, as does the largest of US association, the CFA.

Color terminology varies, too, black sometimes being called ebony, chocolate chestnut, and lilac lavender, and there is some controversy over the cinnamon, caramel, and fawn colors. The showing system in the CFA proved the most

Breakdown of 100 show points

- Color & coat — 50 points
- Head & neck — 15 points
- Body — 15 points
- Ears — 5 points
- Eye shape & setting — 5 points
- Tail — 5 points
- Legs & paws — 5 points

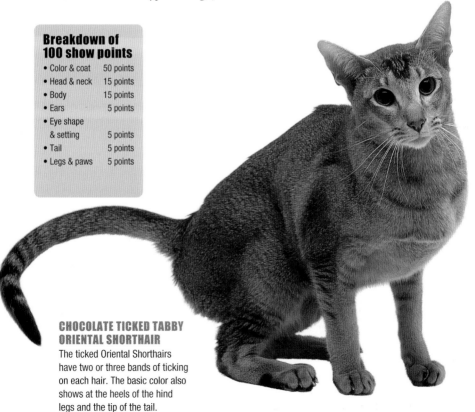

CHOCOLATE TICKED TABBY ORIENTAL SHORTHAIR

The ticked Oriental Shorthairs have two or three bands of ticking on each hair. The basic color also shows at the heels of the hind legs and the tip of the tail.

Key characteristics

Category Foreign shorthair.

Overall build Medium.

Body Long, svelte, and well muscled, but still dainty and elegant. The shoulders should not be wider than the hips.

Colors Black, white, blue, chocolate, lilac, cinnamon, caramel, fawn, red, cream, black tortie, blue tortie, chocolate tortie, lilac tortie, cinnamon tortie, caramel tortie, fawn tortie, black tabby, blue tabby, chocolate tabby, lilac tabby, cinnamon tabby, caramel tabby, fawn tabby, red tabby, cream tabby, silver tabby, black smoke, blue smoke, chocolate smoke, lilac smoke, cinnamon smoke, caramel smoke, fawn smoke, red smoke, black tortie smoke, blue tortie smoke, chocolate tortie smoke, lilac tortie smoke, cinnamon tortie smoke, caramel tortie smoke, black shaded, blue shaded, chocolate shaded, lilac shaded, cameo; torbie: all recognized colors; tipped: all recognized colors.

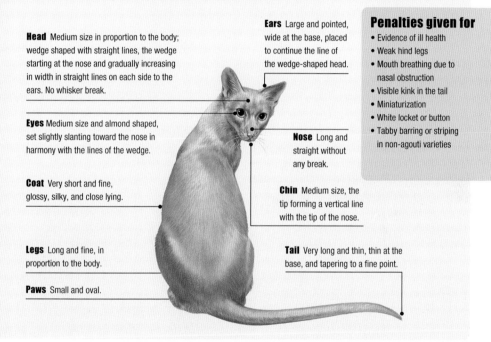

Head Medium size in proportion to the body; wedge shaped with straight lines, the wedge starting at the nose and gradually increasing in width in straight lines on each side to the ears. No whisker break.

Eyes Medium size and almond shaped, set slightly slanting toward the nose in harmony with the lines of the wedge.

Coat Very short and fine, glossy, silky, and close lying.

Legs Long and fine, in proportion to the body.

Paws Small and oval.

Ears Large and pointed, wide at the base, placed to continue the line of the wedge-shaped head.

Nose Long and straight without any break.

Chin Medium size, the tip forming a vertical line with the tip of the nose.

Tail Very long and thin, thin at the base, and tapering to a fine point.

Penalties given for

- Evidence of ill health
- Weak hind legs
- Mouth breathing due to nasal obstruction
- Visible kink in the tail
- Miniaturization
- White locket or button
- Tabby barring or striping in non-agouti varieties

helpful to breeders of Orientals, dividing the breed into five groups: solid colors; shaded; smokes; tabbies; and particolors. In this way Oriental Shorthairs reached championship status level in 1977.

Character and care

The Oriental is extroverted, intelligent, and very affectionate with its own family and friends. It is active and playful, and hates being left alone for long periods.

Orientals are naturally very clean cats, and the short, fine coat can be kept in good condition with daily hand grooming and buffing with a silk scarf. The large ears need regular cleaning, and Orientals should be provided with a scratching post and plenty of toys to play with.

Oriental Shorthair: SOLID VARIETIES

The chocolate-colored Oriental Shorthair is known as the Havana in the UK. It should not be confused with the Havana Brown, which is a different breed with its own characteristics (see page 146).

White

- The coat is pure white without markings or shading of any kind.
- Nose leather and paw pads are pink; eye color is deep, vivid blue. The CFA requires green eyes; blue eyes are also accepted, but odd-eyed cats are not.

Black

- The coat is dense coal black, sound from the roots to the tips of the hair, free from any rusty tinge, and without any white hairs or other markings. There should be no gray undercoat.
- Nose leather is black; paw pads are black or seal brown; eye color is vivid, intense green.

Caramel

- The coat is cool-toned bluish fawn, sound and even throughout without any white hairs, shading, or markings.
- Nose leather and paw pads are bluish fawn; eye color is vivid, intense green.

Fawn

- The coat is warm beige fawn, sound and even throughout without any white hairs, shading, or markings.
- Nose leather is pinkish fawn; paw pads are pink or pinkish fawn; eye color is vivid, intense green.

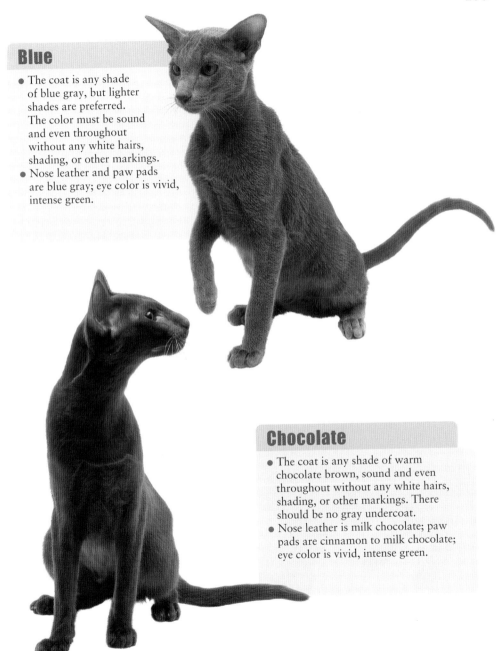

Blue

- The coat is any shade of blue gray, but lighter shades are preferred. The color must be sound and even throughout without any white hairs, shading, or other markings.
- Nose leather and paw pads are blue gray; eye color is vivid, intense green.

Chocolate

- The coat is any shade of warm chocolate brown, sound and even throughout without any white hairs, shading, or other markings. There should be no gray undercoat.
- Nose leather is milk chocolate; paw pads are cinnamon to milk chocolate; eye color is vivid, intense green.

Oriental Shorthair: SOLID VARIETIES

continued

Lilac

- The coat is faded lilac with a slight pinkish tinge, sound and even throughout without any white hairs, shading, or other markings.
- Nose leather and paw pads are lavender pink or faded lilac; eye color is vivid, intense green.

Cinnamon

- The coat is warm cinnamon brown, sound and even throughout without any white hairs, shading, or markings.
- Nose leather is cinnamon brown; paw pads are cinnamon brown to pink; eye color is vivid, intense green.

Red

- The coat is deep, rich, clear and brilliant red, sound and even throughout. Slight shading is allowed on the face and legs, and dark whiskers are permitted.
- Nose leather and paw pads are brick red or pink; eye color is vivid, intense green.

Cream

- The coat is pale, pure pastel cream, with no warm tone, sound and even throughout. Tabby markings may be evident in the coat. Slight shading is allowed on the face and legs, and dark whiskers are permitted.
- Nose leather and paw pads are pink; preferred eye color is vivid, intense green.

Oriental Shorthair:
TORTOISESHELL VARIETIES

With the introduction of the sex-linked gene that produced red and cream colors, litters included female tortoiseshell kittens in various color combinations.

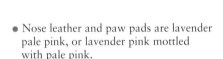

Black tortie

- The coat is black patched or mingled with red and/or light red.
- Nose leather and paw pads are black, brick red, or pink, or black mottled with brick red and/or pink.

Blue tortie

- The coat is light blue gray patched or mingled with pale cream.
- Nose leather and paw pads are blue gray or pink, or blue gray with pink.

Chocolate tortie

- The coat is milk chocolate patched or mingled with red or light red.
- Nose leather is milk chocolate, pale red, or pink, or milk chocolate mottled with pale red and/or pink; paw pads are cinnamon to milk chocolate, pale red, or pink, or cinnamon to milk chocolate mottled with pale red and/or pink.

Lilac tortie

- The coat is faded lilac with a slight pinkish tinge patched or mingled with pale cream.

- Nose leather and paw pads are lavender pale pink, or lavender pink mottled with pale pink.

Cinnamon tortie

- The coat is warm cinnamon brown patched or mingled with red or light red.
- Nose leather and paw pads are cinnamon brown, pinkish red, or pink, or cinnamon brown mottled with pinkish red and/or pink.

Caramel tortie

- The coat is cool-toned bluish fawn patched or mingled with rich beige and/or cream.
- Nose leather and paw pads are bluish fawn or pink, or bluish fawn mottled with pink.

Oriental Shorthair: TABBY VARIETIES

Oriental tabby cats may have any of the following four tabby patterns—classic, mackerel, spotted, or ticked. The markings should be dense and clearly defined and marks on the forehead should form the letter "M."

Chocolate tabby

- The coat, including the lips and chin, is warm fawn, or sandy beige in the ticked tabby, with rich chocolate brown markings. The backs of the legs are chocolate brown.
- Nose leather is chocolate or pale red rimmed with chocolate; paw pads are cinnamon to chocolate; eye color is green.

Black tabby

- The coat is brilliant coppery brown with dense black markings. The lips and chin should be the same color as the rings around the eyes. The backs of the legs are black.
- Nose leather is black or brick red rimmed with black; paw pads are black or seal brown; eye color is green.

Blue tabby

- The coat, including the lips and chin, is pale bluish ivory or warm gray, with markings any shade of blue gray that affords a good contrast. The backs of the legs are a darker blue gray.
- Nose leather is blue or old rose rimmed with blue; paw pads are blue gray or rose; eye color is green.

Lilac tabby

- The coat is off-white to palest lilac, with rich lilac (lilac gray with a pinkish tinge) or lavender markings that afford a good contrast with the base color. The backs of the legs are a darker lilac.
- Nose leather is lavender or pink rimmed with lavender; paw pads are lavender pink; eye color is green.

Oriental Shorthair: TABBY VARIETIES

continued

Caramel tabby

- The coat is cool-toned beige; the markings are a cool-toned bluish fawn; the backs of the legs are a darker bluish fawn.
- Nose leather is bluish fawn or pink rimmed with bluish fawn; paw pads are pink to bluish fawn.

Cinnamon tabby

- The coat is deep apricot with clear, warm, cinnamon brown markings. The backs of the legs are cinnamon brown.
- Nose leather is pale pink; paw pads are cinnamon brown to pinkish brown.

Red tabby

- The coat is red with deep, rich red markings. The backs of the legs are dark red.
- Nose leather is brick red or pink; paw pads are brick red (US) or pink (Europe); eye color is any shade of copper to green, with green preferred.

Silver tabby

- The coat, including the lips and chin, is pure pale silver with dense markings in the main varietal color. The backs of the legs are black.
- Nose leather is black or brick red with black rims; paw pads are black.

Torbie

- In non-dilute colors the coat is patched or mingled with red or light red; the coats of caramel and fawn torbies are patched or mingled with rich beige or cream.
- Nose leather is the varietal color, pink rimmed with the varietal color, or the varietal color mottled with pink; paw pads are the varietal color mottled with pink; eye color is any shade of copper to green (green is preferred).

Cream tabby

- The coat, including the lips and chin, is very pale cream with buff or cream markings that afford a good contrast with the base color. The backs of the legs are dark cream.
- Nose leather and paw pads are pink; eye color is any shade of copper to green (green is preferred).

Fawn tabby

- The coat is dull beige, with markings any shade of beige brown that affords a good contrast with the base color. The backs of the legs are a darker beige fawn.
- Nose leather is pink; paw pads are pinkish fawn.

Oriental Shorthair: TIPPED VARIETIES

The most heavily tipped are the smokes,
the lightest are just called tipped, and the
intermediates are known as shaded.

Shaded

- The hair is tipped to about one third of its length and the undercoat is white, producing the characteristic sparkling appearance of this color group.
- The face and legs may be shaded with tipping.

Smoke

- The hairs are tipped with the appropriate color and have a narrow silvery white band at the roots that can only be seen when the hair is parted.
- In repose, the cat appears to be a solid color, but in motion the silver white undercoat is clearly visible.

Tipped

- The hair is tipped just at its extremity, and the tipping is evenly distributed over the cat's body.
- The face and legs may be tipped, but in adult cats ghost tabby markings are considered a serious fault.

Oriental Shorthair: SEYCHELLOIS

The Seychellois was developed in the UK by a small group of breeders interested in Oriental cats. It is unusual in having a predominantly white coat with splashes of color on the head, legs, and body, and a colored tail.

Seychellois

- Seychellois markings are classified into three groups: Seychellois Neuvième is almost entirely white with a colored tail and a few tiny colored markings on the head; Seychellois Huitième is mainly white with a colored tail and splashes of color on the head and legs; Seychellois Septième is white with a colored tail and splashes of color on the head, legs, and body.
- There is a longhaired Seychellois that is identical in every respect to the shorthaired variety except in its coat, which is of medium length, soft and silky in texture, and longer on the ruff. It has ear tufts and a full, plume-like tail.

Javanese

The longhaired oriental cat, now known as the Javanese, was selectively bred from Oriental Shorthairs and long-coated cats of exceptional oriental type. In the CFA, the name Javanese was given to Balinese cats not conforming to the four main Siamese colors (seal point, blue point, chocolate point, and lilac point). These were the red- and tabby-based colors that in the short-coated varieties are termed Colorpoint Shorthairs by the CFA. In New Zealand, where the red- and tabby- (or lynx-) pointed cats with long coats are accepted, along with the four main Siamese colors, as Balinese, it is the spotted and solid-coated varieties that are called Javanese. In the UK, the CA, as a member of FIFe, accepts all long-coated colors of orientals as Javanese.

SEAL LYNX POINT JAVANESE

The Javanese has the same type and conformation as Siamese and Oriental Shorthairs: long and svelte with fine bones. The coat is fine, silky, and very easy to care for.

Breakdown of 100 show points

• Coat	30 points
• Head	25 points
• Body	25 points
• Eye color	15 points
• Condition	5 points

Key characteristics

Category Semi-longhair (foreign shorthair).
Overall build Medium.
Body Long, svelte, and well muscled, but still dainty. The shoulders should not be wider than the hips.
Colors As for the Oriental Shorthair: black, blue, chocolate, lilac, red, cream, cinnamon, fawn, tortoiseshell (all colors), smoke (all colors), tabby (all colors), torbie (all colors). The eye color for all color varieties is vivid, intense green.

Head Medium size; a long, tapering wedge that starts at the nose and gradually increases in width in straight lines on each side to the ears, with no whisker break in these lines.

Ears Large and pointed, wide at the base, placed to continue the line of the wedge-shaped head.

Eyes Medium size, almond shaped, and set slightly slanted toward the nose.

Nose Long and straight, continuing the line from the forehead without a break.

Coat Fine and silky.

Chin Medium size, with its tip lining up with the nose in the same vertical plane.

Legs Long and fine, in proportion to the body.

Paws Small, dainty, and oval.

Tail Very long and thin, tapering to a fine point, with the hair spreading out like a plume.

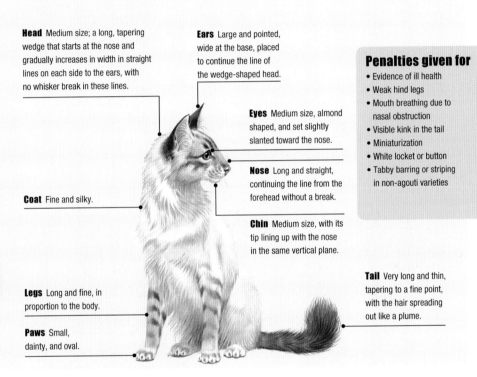

Penalties given for

- Evidence of ill health
- Weak hind legs
- Mouth breathing due to nasal obstruction
- Visible kink in the tail
- Miniaturization
- White locket or button
- Tabby barring or striping in non-agouti varieties

Character and care

Active, always alert, and very inquisitive, the Javanese has an extrovert personality, and is intelligent and quite vocal. It is a very affectionate cat and loves human company, hating to be left alone for long periods.

Regular gentle brushing keeps the coat in good condition; the ruff, underparts, and tail can be combed gently with a broad-toothed comb.

Credits

Quarto Publishing would like to thank all the owners who kindly allowed us to
photograph their cats for inclusion in this book and Rose Forrester for her invaluable
help in researching breed lists and approaching cat owners. All photographs are the
copyright of Quarto.

Katera's book

Emma's
book